WOLFGANG PUCK'S PIZZA, PASTA, AND MORE!

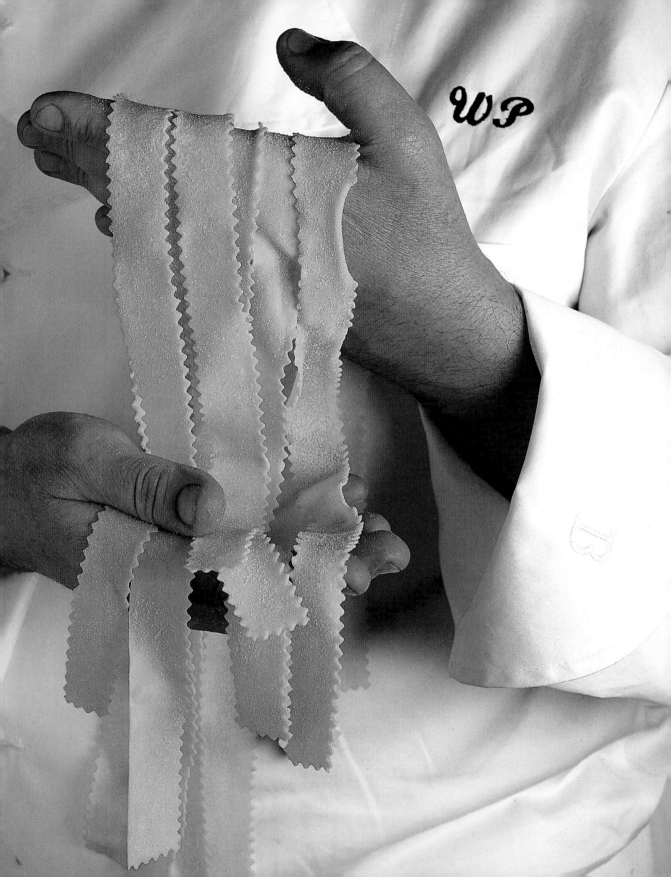

WOLFGANG PUCK'S PIZZA, PASTA, AND MORE!

Wolfgang Puck

PHOTOGRAPHS BY STEVEN ROTHFELD

RANDOM HOUSE NEW YORK

All rights reserved under International and Pan-American Copyright
Conventions. Published in the United States by Random House, Inc.,
New York, and simultaneously in Canada by Random House
of Canada Limited, Toronto.

RANDOM HOUSE and colophon are registered
trademarks of Random House, Inc.

Library of Congress Cataloging-in-Publication Data
Puck, Wolfgang.
Wolfgang Puck's pizza, pasta, and more! / Wolfgang Puck.
        p.   cm.
        ISBN 0-679-43887-4
1. Pizza. 2. Cookery (Pasta) I. Title: Pizza, pasta, and more!. II. Title.
    TX770.P58 P83 2000   641.8′22—dc21   00-038715

Printed in the United States of America on acid-free paper
Random House website address: www.atrandom.com

2 4 6 8 9 7 5 3

First Edition

This book is dedicated to my two sons, Cameron and Byron, who enjoy eating pasta and pizzas but enjoy making them even more.

To my wife, Barbara, whose passion, dedication, and love make her the centerpiece of my life.

To my mother, Maria, who, at seventy-five, still amazes me with her energy and talent in the kitchen.

To Judy Gethers, who has more patience than any one of us. Without her, this book would still be typed pages in a drawer somewhere.

To Lee Hefter, a very talented chef who not only inspires me but also inspires a big group of young chefs in our Spago kitchen.

Awaiting the stars' arrival at the Shrine Auditorium.

ACKNOWLEDGMENTS

With sincere thanks to:

David Robins, who is not only a great cook but also a smart businessman.

To Mitch and Steve Rosenthal—I always feel like I'm their third brother.

To François Kwaku-Dongo, who taught me the subtleties of a great risotto.

To Matt Bencivenga, who makes the Spago kitchen run like a Swiss watch.

To Robin Stotter and all the wonderful people at the Wolfgang Puck Cafés.

To Jennifer Jasinski.

To Michael French, who made big strides as chef at Spago Palo Alto.

To Gina de Cew and Jennifer Naylor.

To Luis and Rene, our new chefs at Chinois.

To our managing partner, Tom Kaplan.

To Klaus and Amanda in Chicago.

To Bella Lanstman, the supreme commander of Chinois, and more important, a wonderful friend.

To Mark Ferguson, a very talented Italian chef with an American name.

To Joseph Bennett and John La Grone.

To all the chefs, sous chefs, and cooks in our restaurants and cafés.

Thanks to Pamela Cannon for her perseverance in getting this book done.

To Steven Rothfeld for his wonderful photography.

To Georgiana Goodwin for her excellent design work and Teri Gelber for her fine-tuning.

To the Chino family, who in their search for the best never fail to amaze me.

Special thanks to Cecilia de Castro and her team of tasters, testers, and writers, and to Maggie Boone, without whom these pages would be blank.

CONTENTS

SALADS AND SOUPS

PIZZA

PASTA

Not long ago, my wife, Barbara, and I and our two boys were trying to decide where to go for dinner. Barbara was in the mood for Japanese food, but the boys protested and said they would much rather stay home—they wanted pasta for dinner.

It occurred to me, as the boys begged for pasta, how rarely I get to eat with my family at home. When you're in the business I'm in, you work most evenings, and when you aren't at the restaurant, you often don't have time to plan dinner. So, granting the boys their request, I changed back into my work clothes, put on an apron, and started to dig through the cupboards and refrigerator. Cameron and Byron watched in anticipation as I put the water on to boil for pasta and began washing the vegetables for the salad. As they quizzed me about each step—why I salted the water, how to tell when the noodles are ready—I remembered watching my mother when I was a boy and asking the exact same questions. Eating is something we all must do and something almost all of us enjoy. And cooking together gives us a connection to one another. When the meal was ready and we all sat down together to eat, I thought to myself, Life just doesn't get better than this.

Eating with family and friends is like having a little party. It is pure pleasure, a relaxing and fun experience. When I set out to write this book, I envisioned a collection that would be accessible to everyone, one that would be fun to cook from and filled with simple and wonderful dishes that wouldn't require elaborate ingredients and complicated techniques. Casual and easy to prepare, these are dishes everyone can make and enjoy.

Years ago, when I cooked in the south of France, most of the dishes we prepared were regional. Many of the ingredients were grown or cultivated locally, whether it was the vegetables, the fish, or the cheese. When I opened the first Spago in Los Angeles in 1982, my philosophy was influenced by those years in the south of France. I believed that, whenever possible, a restaurant should represent the place where it is located. Los Angeles, with such a wonderful Mediterranean climate, was the ideal place to open a restaurant. Like southern France, the California climate allowed for a full year of growing, with season after season of incredible fruits and vegetables. As I learned more about this exotic city, I was amazed by all of the different ethnic foods it had to offer. I was already well versed in French and Italian cooking and drew from them when I cooked. But living in Los Angeles, I also discovered Japanese, Chinese, Thai, and Mexican ingredients, which eventually found their way into my kitchen. I never wanted to imitate these cuisines as much as to try to combine them in a fresh new way, much like the fusion cuisine movement of the late nineties.

The ingredients should be the star of the show in your kitchen. Expensive, shiny pots and pans only go sc far; a dish can only be as good as its ingredients. Few professional cooks can make something taste great using second-rate products. Stick to seasonal foods if you want the fullest flavors. For the best indication of what's in season, go to your local farmer's market and see what's selling. I'm shocked when I see corn soup on a restaurant menu in the middle of winter. Where are they getting this corn? It certainly came from the freezer, not the fields. Let your ingredients guide you, and don't be afraid to improvise. Don't get too attached to the exact ingredients in a recipe. If you can't find that specific ingredient, improvise or find another recipe that calls for fruits and vegetables in season. If you start out with good ingredients and follow a few simple directions, you are guaranteed a delicious outcome.

Shop wisely for your ingredients, and don't be fooled by the price of something. Price doesn't always determine quality. At the fish market, there may be fresh squid for only two dollars a pound and frozen scallops at twelve dollars a pound. I would choose the fresh squid over the frozen scallops, and by doing so I save money and get a superior product. Develop a relationship with your butcher or fishmonger and ask questions, the way we do at the restaurant. You must be savvy and demand the best from your grocers.

In the 1980s, I was fortunate to meet and befriend the Chino family. Their family farm is one of the wonders of the world. Using only organic growing methods, they have reintroduced many heirloom and lost varieties back into the agriculture and food community. When I first tasted Chino tomatoes I couldn't believe the intense, sweet flavors. Their tomatoes were as delicious as the ones in my mother's garden in Austria, and there were row after row of strange and unique varieties I had never heard of. The corn was like nothing I had ever tried: sweet, tender, the best. That was back in the days when we chefs couldn't get good produce unless we went directly to the source. There were no farmer's markets in the city. To spend more time there, I would plan my vacations in San Diego County, just to be near their farm. My evenings were spent in amazement, cooking and eating those incredible vegetables. Being around the land and the farmers felt comfortable. The farmers care so much for the food, and we do our best not to change the flavors but to enhance them.

So many chefs these days are forced to become overly involved in the business side of running their restaurants. They barely have time to look around in the markets or talk with their vendors to see what ingredients are best. I'm the most content when I'm in the kitchen. I like to see the raw food and touch it, to experience the cooking process from the beginning to the end. From the shopping, chopping, and cooking to the first bite at the table, being involved with the food is the most rewarding experience.

Most of us lead extremely busy lives. Nowadays we travel more, we work longer during the week, and we play harder, too. With such fast-paced lives, I think sometimes we forget about the basics. Simple things, like dinnertime with our children, don't hold priority any longer. Or making supper for your neighbor or friend, instead of ordering out. These are pleasures that we must not forget. I hope that these recipes will inspire you to go back to the kitchen and enjoy the experience. Though my cooking and recipes are always evolving and changing, these are some of the favorites that have weathered time—favorites of mine, my family, and my customers.

WOLFGANG PUCK'S

Catching up on phone calls between courses.

THE BASICS

Stocks,
Sauces, Dressings,
and
Condiments

CHICKEN STOCK

When bones, vegetables, and herbs are allowed to simmer for several hours, the flavors meld together into one exuberant broth, or stock. All great chefs will tell you that without a good stock, your final dish will suffer. At home, people sometimes resort to water as a liquid base because they don't have stock ready. Depending on the dish, water will usually take flavor out instead of putting it in.

Good stock comes from good ingredients. Never throw away chicken bones! The next time you buy a whole chicken, have the butcher bone it, and take the bones home to use for stock. The longer you reduce your stock, the more concentrated it becomes. Make a few different types of stocks and keep them in small containers or plastic bags in the freezer.

MAKES ABOUT 2 QUARTS

5 to 6 pounds chicken bones, including necks and feet, coarsely chopped

1 medium carrot, peeled, trimmed, and cut into 1-inch slices

1 medium onion, peeled, trimmed, and quartered

1 small celery stalk, trimmed and cut into 1-inch slices

1 small leek, cleaned, trimmed, and cut into 1-inch slices

1 sprig of fresh thyme

3 sprigs of fresh parsley with stems

1 bay leaf

$\frac{1}{2}$ teaspoon whole white peppercorns

1.   Place the chicken bones in a 6- or 7-quart pot, pour cold water over to cover, and bring to a rolling boil. Skim off the foam and fat that collects on the top.

2.   Add the remaining ingredients, lower the heat to a simmer, and simmer uncovered for 2 to 3 hours, skimming as necessary. Strain through a fine-mesh strainer into a clean bowl and cool. Refrigerate, covered, for up to 3 days, discarding the hardened layer of fat before using or freezing.

TO PREPARE AHEAD: Through step 2. The stock can be frozen in small quantities for up to 3 months and reheated and used as needed.

NOTE: To make Brown Chicken Stock, preheat the oven to 400°F. Spread the bones and slices of 1 medium onion in a roasting pan and set in the oven. Turn the bones to brown all sides until they are a deep golden brown, about 30 minutes. Do not allow them to burn, since that will give the stock a bitter taste. Transfer the bones and onion to the stockpot, and place the roasting pan on the stove. Over medium heat, deglaze the pan with 2 cups of water, scraping up all the bits that stick to the bottom of the pan. Pour into the stockpot and add 3 quarts of water. Bring to a boil, lower heat, and simmer for 3 hours. Strain into a clean stockpot and boil for 20 to 30 minutes, until the stock is reduced to 2 cups. At this point, the stock is more concentrated and more flavorful. Strain into a clean bowl and cool. Since brown stock is primarily a base for sauces and only a small amount is used, pour the cooled stock into an ice-cube tray. When completely solid, release the cubes, enclose in a plastic bag, and return to the freezer. When needed, one or two cubes can be defrosted and used.

VEGETABLE STOCK

For those who prefer not to eat meat, this can be substituted for a meat stock when making sauces.

MAKES ABOUT 7 CUPS

2 tablespoons extra-virgin olive oil

2 heads garlic (about 4 ounces), each cut in half horizontally

2 medium white onions (1¼ pounds), peeled, trimmed, and diced

2 or 3 large tomatoes (1¼ pounds), cut into quarters

1 large fennel bulb (1 pound), peeled and cut into 2-inch pieces

2 medium zucchini (¾ pound), trimmed and cut into 2-inch pieces

3 celery stalks (about 4 ounces), roughly chopped

2 carrots (about 4 ounces), peeled, trimmed, and cut into 2-inch pieces

3 tablespoons tomato paste

1 bay leaf

2 sprigs each of fresh thyme, flat-leaf parsley, and basil, tied into a bundle

1 tablespoon kosher salt

Freshly ground white pepper

Pinch of sugar

1. In a 4- or 5-quart stockpot, heat the olive oil. Over medium heat, sauté the garlic, cut-side down, until it starts to brown. Add all the vegetables, the tomato paste, the bay leaf, the bundle of herbs, and the salt. Cook for about 5 minutes, stirring to coat with a little of the oil, then pour in enough boiling water to cover the vegetables. Simmer, uncovered, until the vegetables are very tender and the stock is flavorful, about 45 minutes.

2. Strain through a fine-mesh strainer, mashing down on the vegetables to extract all the flavor possible. Season with a little white pepper and sugar. Adjust the seasoning, adding more salt and pepper as necessary.

3. Use as needed.

TO PREPARE AHEAD: Through step 2, the stock can be made and refrigerated for 2 or 3 days. It also can be frozen for up to 3 months and used as needed.

BROWN VEAL STOCK

MAKES ABOUT 2 QUARTS

8 pounds veal bones (or veal and beef bones), cut into 2-inch chunks

2 medium onions, peeled, trimmed, and coarsely chopped

2 medium carrots, peeled, trimmed, and coarsely chopped

1 celery stalk, peeled, trimmed, and coarsely chopped

1 leek, cleaned, trimmed, and coarsely chopped

2 large tomatoes, quartered*

1 teaspoon whole black peppercorns

2 bay leaves

2 sprigs of fresh thyme

About 8 garlic cloves, peeled and crushed, optional

1.   Preheat the oven to 450°F.

2.   Arrange the bones in a roasting pan large enough to hold them in a single layer. Roast in the oven until dark golden brown, about 1½ hours, turning to brown all sides. After 1 hour, add the remaining ingredients to brown.

3.   Transfer the bones and vegetables to a large 10- to 12-quart stockpot. Pour off the fat from the roasting pan and deglaze the pan with 2 cups of water, scraping up any particles that stick to the bottom of the pan. Pour into the stockpot with enough additional water to cover the ingredients by 2 inches. Bring the water to a boil, reduce the heat, and simmer, uncovered, 5 to 6 hours, skimming off any foam and fat that forms on the top.

---

*In the winter, when tomatoes are not at their best, you can use ½ cup tomato paste.

4.   Strain the liquid into a clean pot, pressing down to extract all the juices. Reduce, over medium heat, until about 2 quarts remain. (If you want a more concentrated flavor, reduce to 1 quart and use more sparingly.)

5.   Cool and refrigerate in a covered container for up to 3 days, discarding any hardened layer of fat before using or freezing.

TO PREPARE AHEAD: Through step 5. The stock can be frozen in ice-cube trays. When solid, release from the trays, enclose in a well-sealed plastic bag, and return to the freezer.

BROWN DUCK STOCK

The brown stock adds color as well as flavor to any sauce that calls for stock. You can combine chicken and duck bones if necessary. Freeze the bones, and when you have enough, make the stock.

MAKES ABOUT 1½ QUARTS

⁂

7 pounds duck bones (backs, legs, and breasts)

2 large onions (about 1½ pounds), peeled, trimmed, and coarsely chopped

2 large carrots (about ½ pound), peeled, trimmed, and coarsely chopped

3 celery stalks (about ½ pound), trimmed and coarsely chopped

¼ cup tomato paste

1 teaspoon whole black peppercorns

2 bay leaves

2 sprigs of fresh thyme

1.   Preheat the oven to 400°F.

2.   Arrange the duck bones in a large roasting pan and roast until brown, turning

to brown all sides. When golden, add the vegetables to brown. This entire procedure should take about 1½ hours.

3.   Transfer the bones and vegetables to a large stockpot and stir in the tomato paste. Pour off the fat from the roasting pan and deglaze the pan with 2 cups of water, scraping up any bits that cling to the pan. Pour into the stockpot with just enough additional water to cover the bones. Add the peppercorns, bay leaves, and thyme. Bring to a boil, lower the heat, and simmer, uncovered, for 4 to 5 hours, skimming off any foam and fat that form on the top.

4.   Strain into a clean pot, pressing down on the bones and vegetables to extract all the juices. Cook over low heat until approximately 6 cups remain, about 1 hour longer.

5.   Cool and refrigerate in a covered container for up to 3 days, discarding any hardened layer of fat before using or freezing.

TO PREPARE AHEAD: Through step 4. The stock can be frozen and reheated when needed. As with the other stocks, this too can be reduced still further, to concentrate the flavor, and frozen in ice-cube trays.

HAZELNUT BROWN BUTTER AND HERB SAUCE

Hazelnuts have a unique and unmistakable flavor. Whether you're making Sweet Potato or Spinach and Wild Mushroom Ravioli (see pages 193 and 191), this buttery sauce is the perfect finishing touch. To serve with chicken, add a tablespoon of balsamic vinegar, or with fish, simply add a tablespoon or two of lemon juice. Be sure you cook the butter until it's well browned and the kitchen is filled with that toasty, nutty aroma of browning butter.

MAKES ABOUT 1½ CUPS

1 cup hazelnuts

8 tablespoons (1 stick) unsalted butter, cut into small pieces

2¼ cups homemade Chicken Stock (see page 4) or store-bought, heated

1½ teaspoons chopped fresh thyme leaves

1½ teaspoons chopped fresh oregano leaves

½ teaspoon kosher salt

½ teaspoon freshly ground black pepper

1 tablespoon freshly grated Parmesan cheese

1. Preheat the oven to 350°F. Arrange the hazelnuts on a medium baking tray and toast for 10 to 12 minutes, turning after 5 minutes. (This can be done in a toaster oven.) Remove to a clean towel and rub to remove as much of the skin as possible. Chop coarsely and set aside.

2. Make the sauce: Heat a 10-inch skillet. Over medium heat, melt the butter, constantly moving the pan in circular motions so that the butter browns evenly. When the butter gives off a fragrant, nutty aroma, it should be ready. Watch carefully to prevent the butter from burning.

3. Add the stock, thyme, oregano, salt, and pepper and reduce the sauce by half. At this point, add the cooked pasta of your choice to heat through. Remove from the heat and stir in the chopped hazelnuts and the Parmesan cheese. Serve immediately.

TO PREPARE AHEAD: Through step 1.

OVEN-DRIED-TOMATO, BASIL, AND PARMESAN CHEESE SAUCE

If using sun-dried tomatoes rather than oven-dried, the tomatoes should be oil-packed. This very simple sauce not only goes well with pasta or rice, but it can be spooned over baked chicken or used as a sauce with meatballs.

MAKES ABOUT 1⅓ CUPS

4 tablespoons (½ stick) unsalted butter, cut into pieces

1 teaspoon minced garlic

¼ cup Oven-Dried Tomatoes (see page 26), cut into large strips

2 cups homemade Chicken Stock (see page 4) or store-bought, heated

¼ teaspoon kosher salt

¼ teaspoon freshly ground black pepper

¼ cup chopped fresh basil leaves

2 tablespoons freshly grated Parmesan cheese

1.   Heat a medium saucepan over medium heat. Add the butter, and when it is bubbling, add the garlic. Reduce the heat to low and sweat the garlic for 1 or 2 minutes. Add the tomatoes, stir through, and then pour in the stock. Add the salt and pepper, increase the heat to medium-high, and reduce the stock by about half. When it is almost reduced, lower the heat and add the basil.

2.   If combining with pasta, add 8 ounces of cooked pasta of your choice to the pan and heat through. If the sauce is too thick, thin with a bit more stock. Remove the sauce from the heat and stir the Parmesan cheese into the pan. (If you add the cheese while the sauce is still cooking, the cheese tends to stick to the pan.) Adjust the seasoning to taste.

TO PREPARE AHEAD: Through step 1, reducing almost halfway. When ready to serve, warm the sauce over low heat.

ROASTED GARLIC AND HERB SAUCE

This is a simple sauce that can easily be served over cooked chicken, sautéed shrimp, or leftover pork or beef.

MAKES ABOUT 2 CUPS

1½ heads (about 6 ounces) garlic cloves, peeled

1½ tablespoons extra-virgin olive oil

2½ cups homemade Chicken Stock (see page 4) or store-bought, heated

Kosher salt and freshly ground black pepper

¼ cup chopped fresh flat-leaf parsley leaves

2 tablespoons chopped fresh thyme leaves

1½ teaspoons chopped fresh oregano leaves

5 tablespoons unsalted butter, cut into small pieces

1. Preheat the oven to 350°F.

2. In a small ovenproof pan, toss the garlic cloves in the olive oil to coat well. Roast until the garlic is light golden brown and tender, about 15 minutes, turning occasionally so that the cloves brown evenly.

3. Transfer the garlic to a blender, pour in the stock, and season lightly with salt and pepper. Process until smooth. Add the chopped herbs and the butter and continue to process until smooth. Transfer to a container and allow to cool. If made early in the day, refrigerate, covered, until needed.

4. When ready to serve, reheat the sauce over low heat.

TO PREPARE AHEAD: Through step 3.

TOMATO GARLIC BASIL SAUCE

This sauce is extremely versatile. It is delicious on pasta, and it can be used when making lasagna. The recipe can be doubled or tripled, and if you like a sauce with texture, you can eliminate the straining in Step 1. Without the butter, it can be spread over pizza dough before layering with additional ingredients.

MAKES ABOUT 2½ CUPS

2 tablespoons extra-virgin olive oil

1 small onion, peeled, trimmed, and minced

3 garlic cloves, minced

1 tablespoon tomato paste

2 pounds Roma tomatoes, peeled, seeded, and diced

1 cup homemade Chicken Stock (see page 4) or store-bought, heated

6 to 8 fresh basil leaves, washed and dried

6 tablespoons (¾ stick) unsalted butter, cut into small pieces

Kosher salt and freshly ground black pepper

1.   In a medium saucepan, heat the olive oil. Over medium-high heat, sauté the onion just until wilted, 4 to 5 minutes. Add the garlic and cook 1 minute longer. Add the tomato paste, then the tomatoes, cook 2 or 3 minutes, and pour in the chicken stock. Reduce until the sauce thickens, 15 to 20 minutes. Strain into a clean saucepan.

2.   Cut the basil leaves into a chiffonade* and stir into the sauce. Whisk in the butter, piece by piece, and season to taste with salt and pepper. Keep warm.

TO PREPARE AHEAD: Through step 2. Cool and refrigerate, covered, until needed. Reheat over low heat.

---

*To make a chiffonade, stack 2 or 3 basil leaves, roll the stack lengthwise, and slice the roll crosswise into thin strips. Repeat until you have the necessary amount.

PESTO

This recipe can be doubled very easily. At Spago we use a sweet olive oil, not too sharp and overwhelming, found in the Emilia-Romagna region of Italy. This can be brushed over pizzas and fish, and it turns a simple pasta into something special. In Italy, pesto is generally made with a mortar and pestle, which probably accounts for the name, but it can also be done in a blender, so you will find both methods below.

MAKES A SCANT ¼ CUP

12 medium fresh basil leaves, washed, dried, and coarsely chopped

3 medium garlic cloves, coarsely chopped

2 tablespoons pine nuts, lightly toasted

Pinch of salt

3 tablespoons extra-virgin olive oil

1.   In a mortar and pestle, pound the basil, garlic, nuts, and salt until thoroughly mashed. Add the oil, a few drops at a time, until you have a smooth paste.

2.   Pesto can also be made in a blender. Pour in the oil first, then the garlic, nuts, and finally the basil leaves. Blend on low to a smooth paste. Season with the kosher salt.

TO PREPARE AHEAD: Pesto can be prepared and refrigerated or frozen. Bring to room temperature before using.

If you own a mortar and pestle, use it to make this Pesto. You'll definitely notice the difference in flavor when the fresh herbs are stone-ground.

WILD MUSHROOM SAUCE

The Mushroom Base intensifies the mushroom flavor of this sauce. The sauce can be spooned over almost any pasta of your choice, but it is delectable with the Spinach and Wild Mushroom Ravioli on page 191.

MAKES 1½ CUPS

4 tablespoons (½ stick) unsalted butter, cut into small pieces

10 ounces mixed wild mushrooms (such as morels, shiitake, porcini), stemmed (stems reserved for soups), larger mushrooms cut as necessary into bite-size pieces

1½ teaspoons minced garlic

1½ teaspoons minced shallots

3 cups homemade Chicken Stock (see page 4) or store-bought

½ teaspoon kosher salt

½ teaspoon freshly ground black pepper

2 teaspoons Mushroom Base (see page 133), optional

3 tablespoons chopped fresh flat-leaf parsley leaves

3 tablespoons freshly grated Parmesan cheese

Truffle oil, optional

1.   In a large skillet or wide saucepan, melt the butter over medium heat. Add the mushrooms, garlic, and shallots and stir to coat with the melted butter. Lower the heat, cover, and sweat the mushrooms for 1 or 2 minutes.

2.   Raise the heat to medium-high. Add the stock, salt, and pepper. For additional flavor, the Mushroom Base can be added at this point. Reduce until the sauce has thickened slightly.

3.   When ready to serve with the pasta of your choice, add the parsley and Parmesan cheese. If desired, a few drops of truffle oil can be swirled through. Adjust the seasoning to taste.

TO PREPARE AHEAD: Have all the ingredients ready and cook as needed. The sauce can be made ahead through step 2 and refrigerated until ready to use later in the day. Finished sauce can be kept frozen for up to 1 month.

Every type of mushroom has its own distinct flavor. Sometimes I like to put trumpet, crimini, and morels all in one dish.

SPAGO HOUSE DRESSING

Every restaurant and every household should have its very own house dressing. Choose your favorite oil and vinegar and feel free to add a variety of herbs and spices. Always keep a batch mixed up in the refrigerator to dress a salad, drizzle over fresh tomatoes, or brush over the Cheeseless Pizza (page 99).

MAKES ABOUT 1 CUP

3 tablespoons balsamic vinegar

1 tablespoon sherry wine vinegar

1 tablespoon Dijon mustard

1/2 tablespoon minced fresh thyme leaves

1 small shallot, minced

1/2 cup extra-virgin olive oil

1/3 cup walnut oil (or part walnut and part hazelnut oil)

1/4 teaspoon kosher salt

1/8 teaspoon freshly ground white pepper

1. In a medium bowl, whisk together the balsamic and sherry wine vinegars, the Dijon mustard, minced thyme, and the minced shallot. Slowly whisk in the oils and when emulsified, season with the salt and pepper. Refrigerate in a covered container.

2. When ready to use, whisk again.

TO PREPARE AHEAD: Through step 1, the dressing will keep 3 to 4 weeks.

CHILI OIL

MAKES 1 CUP

1 cup peanut or extra-virgin olive oil   *¼ cup red pepper flakes*

In a small saucepan, heat the oil to a simmer. Stir in the red pepper flakes and re-move the pan from the heat. Cool. Store in a covered jar and refrigerate until needed.

TO PREPARE AHEAD: Chili oil will keep, refrigerated, for 3 to 4 weeks.

Plating 5,000 appetizers is easier said than done.

CHILI AND GARLIC OIL

Brush this flavorful oil on pizza dough or blend it into pasta dough. It can also be used for sautéing ingredients for pastas.

MAKES ABOUT 2 CUPS

1 whole head garlic (about 2½ ounces), cloves separated and peeled

2 cups extra-virgin olive oil

1 tablespoon red pepper flakes

1.   In a small saucepan, combine the garlic cloves and olive oil and bring to a boil. Reduce the heat and simmer until the garlic turns golden brown, 10 to 15 minutes. (Do not let the garlic get too dark because the oil will have a bitter taste.)

2.   Let cool and then add the red pepper flakes. Infuse for at least 2 hours to allow the flavors to blend. Refrigerate in a covered container.

TO PREPARE AHEAD: Through step 2, oil will last 2 to 3 weeks.

BALSAMIC REDUCTION

A few drops of this reduction will add flavor to almost any green salad. Of course, the better the vinegar, the better the taste.

MAKES ⅓ CUP

---※---

1 cup balsamic vinegar

1. Pour the vinegar into a small saucepan and on very low heat reduce to ⅓ cup. Be careful not to reduce too much. As the vinegar cools, it thickens.

2. Refrigerate in a covered container and use as needed.

TO PREPARE AHEAD: Through step 2, the vinegar will last for up to 2 weeks.

BLACK AND GREEN OLIVE TAPENADE

The tapenade can be served as an hors d'oeuvre, in a small bowl, surrounded with tiny toasted bread slices or crackers. At Spago, we spread goat cheese onto lightly toasted croutons, top them with the tapenade, and serve them with our Caesar Salad (see page 38).

MAKES 1 HEAPING CUP

---

1 cup Niçoise olives, pitted

1 cup small green French olives (Picholine), pitted

1/4 cup Oven-Dried Tomatoes (see page 26), drained

1 tablespoon capers

1 garlic clove

1 anchovy fillet

1/2 tablespoon chopped fresh basil leaves

1/2 tablespoon chopped fresh thyme leaves

1/2 tablespoon chopped fresh flat-leaf parsley leaves

1/4 tablespoon chopped fresh oregano leaves

1/4 cup extra-virgin olive oil

In a food processor, combine all the ingredients except the olive oil. Using the pulse button, process until coarsely chopped and well blended. Continue to process, slowly adding the olive oil. Refrigerate in a covered container. Use as needed.

TO PREPARE AHEAD: Tapenade will keep up to 1 week, refrigerated, in a covered container.

Niçoise olives and Provençal green olives combine with fresh herbs and oven-dried tomatoes for a delicious tapenade.

CAESAR VINAIGRETTE

MAKES ABOUT 2 CUPS

1 egg

3 tablespoons fresh lemon juice

1 tablespoon minced garlic

½ teaspoon Worcestershire sauce

¼ teaspoon red pepper flakes

1 tablespoon Dijon mustard

2 anchovy fillets, mashed

Scant cup peanut oil

⅓ cup extra-virgin olive oil

¼ cup freshly grated Parmesan cheese

Kosher salt and freshly ground black pepper

In a medium bowl, whisk together the egg, lemon juice, garlic, Worcestershire sauce, red pepper flakes, mustard, and anchovies. Slowly whisk in the oils to emulsify. Stir in the cheese and season with salt and pepper. Refrigerate in a covered container. When ready to use, whisk again.

TO PREPARE AHEAD: Caesar Vinaigrette will keep up to 1 week, refrigerated, in a covered container.

SPICED CARAMELIZED PECANS

The nuts have a sweet and spicy taste, a very delicious combination. We toss them over our green salad for flavor and texture, but the nuts are almost too good to save just for salads.

MAKES 2 CUPS

* * *

3 cups peanut oil

2 cups pecan halves

1 teaspoon kosher salt

1/2 teaspoon cayenne pepper

1 cup sifted confectioners' sugar

1. In a deep-fryer or a deep pot, heat the oil to 350°F. (A deep-frying thermometer can be clipped to the side of the pan so that you can tell when the proper temperature has been reached.)

2. Meanwhile, in a large saucepan bring 2 quarts of water to a boil. Add the pecans and boil for 2 minutes. Drain in a large strainer, shaking off all excess water. Sprinkle the salt and cayenne pepper over the nuts and then coat with the confectioners' sugar, a little at a time, allowing the sugar to melt into the pecans. Toss the nuts by shaking the strainer, adding a little more sugar each time, until all the sugar is used and all the nuts are coated. Do not use hands or a spoon to toss. The nuts should have a glaze of sugar.

3. Carefully add the nuts to the heated oil, keeping the oil at 350°. Cook until golden brown, about 3 minutes, stirring occasionally. Remove with a slotted spoon to a baking tray to cool.

TO PREPARE AHEAD: Through step 3, the nuts can be stored in an airtight container and will keep for up to 1 week.

HERBED GOAT CHEESE

Herbed goat cheese can be added to pasta or pizza, but it also can be served on toasted rounds with salad or soup. If you prefer certain herbs, by all means combine your favorites to roll onto the cheese.

MAKES ONE 7- OR 8-OUNCE LOG

2 teaspoons chopped fresh flat-leaf parsley leaves

2 teaspoons chopped fresh chives

1 teaspoon chopped fresh thyme leaves

½ teaspoon freshly ground black pepper

One 7- or 8-ounce log of goat cheese

Combine the parsley, chives, thyme, and pepper and place on a flat surface. Roll the log of cheese in the mixture, coating all sides and retaining the shape of the log. Wrap in plastic wrap and refrigerate until needed.

OVEN-DRIED TOMATOES

For the best and tastiest result, these should be prepared when the tomatoes are in their prime. The recipe can be doubled or tripled if desired.

MAKES 1¼ CUPS

About 12 medium Roma tomatoes (2 pounds)

½ cup extra-virgin olive oil, plus additional as needed

1 teaspoon minced fresh thyme leaves

6 garlic cloves, crushed

½ teaspoon kosher salt

¼ teaspoon freshly ground black pepper

½ teaspoon sugar

1. Preheat the oven to 250°F.

2. In a pot of boiling water, blanch tomatoes. Drain and refresh in ice water. Drain. Peel, core, cut into quarters, and remove seeds.

3. Line a baking tray with parchment paper and arrange the tomato quarters on the tray, cut side down. Drizzle generously with olive oil. Sprinkle with thyme and garlic. In a small bowl, combine salt, pepper, and sugar, and sprinkle evenly over the tomatoes.

4. Bake until the tomatoes begin to shrivel, about 1 hour. When the tomatoes are cool enough to handle, transfer to a container. Pour olive oil over and cover the container. Refrigerate and use as needed.

TO PREPARE AHEAD: The tomatoes will keep 2 to 3 days, refrigerated, in a covered container.

CARAMELIZED ONIONS

Sprinkle the onions over pizza, over pasta, even over mashed potatoes.
These will add wonderful flavor to many dishes.

MAKES ABOUT ¾ CUP

2 tablespoons extra-virgin olive oil

1 large red, yellow, or white onion
(¾ pound), peeled, trimmed, and cut
into ¾-inch dice

2 tablespoons balsamic vinegar

Kosher salt and freshly ground black
pepper

1. In a 10-inch skillet or sauté pan, heat the oil. Add the onion and cook over medium heat, stirring frequently, until *lightly* browned, about 15 minutes. Add the vinegar and cook 1 minute longer. Season with salt and pepper to taste.

2. Cool the onion and transfer to a covered container. Refrigerate and use as needed.

TO PREPARE AHEAD: Through step 2, reheating over low heat.

BALSAMIC GLAZED SHALLOTS

The glazed shallots can go in pastas and on pizzas, giving an added zing to the other ingredients. Try to buy shallots that are the same size. If some are too large, you can cut them.

MAKES ABOUT 2 CUPS

1 pound shallots

3 tablespoons extra-vigin olive oil

1 tablespoon unsalted butter

1½ cups balsamic vinegar

1. Peel the shallots, and cut them in half or in quarters so that you have pieces about 1 inch wide.

2. In a 10- or 12-inch skillet, heat the oil. Add the shallots and over medium heat, sauté the shallots until golden brown on both sides. Carefully turn with tongs so that the shallots remain as much in one piece as possible. Reduce the heat and add the butter. When the butter has melted, deglaze the pan with the vinegar and reduce by half.

3. Preheat the oven (or toaster oven) to 400°F.

4. Transfer the contents of the skillet to a small baking pan, cover with aluminum foil, and bake 10 to 12 minutes. The shallots should be tender but still slightly crunchy.

5. Use as needed.

TO PREPARE AHEAD: Through step 4, cool and refrigerate, covered.

DOUBLE-BLANCHED GARLIC

There are various ways to sweeten garlic and remove some of the bite. This is one way—very simple, very quick, and very effective. The cloves should be tender but still crunchy.

AS NEEDED

Garlic

Kosher salt

1. Have a bowl of ice water ready.

2. Remove the ends of the desired number of garlic cloves. In a small saucepan, pour in enough water to cover the garlic. Salt lightly and bring to a boil. Carefully drop the whole cloves into the water and blanch for 30 seconds.

3. Remove the cloves with a slotted spoon and immediately plunge into the ice water to stop the cooking process.

4. Repeat the process, again cooling the garlic by plunging it into the ice water. Drain the garlic and dry it well. The peels should slip off easily. Cut the garlic into slices and use as needed.

TO PREPARE AHEAD: The garlic can be prepared up to 2 days ahead and refrigerated in a covered container.

It takes lots of hands to get all this food out at once.

ROASTED GARLIC

Here is the first of two methods you can use for roasting garlic (the second method follows). In this one the garlic is peeled and the individual cloves are roasted. The cloves can then be sliced and tossed with your favorite pasta dish or sprinkled over cooked fish or vegetables.

In the second method, the whole head of garlic is roasted. The garlic pulp is then removed and stirred into vegetables and soups, mashed into potatoes, and, of course, added to most pastas and pizzas.

For both methods, the garlic can be roasted in a small pan in a toaster oven. For garlic lovers, roasting is a must—it makes the garlic sweeter, more buttery, and tastier.

MAKES ABOUT 1 CUP

5 to 6 ounces peeled and trimmed garlic cloves

2 tablespoons Chili and Garlic Oil (see page 20)

1.   Preheat the oven to 375°F.

2.   Putting them in a small roasting pan, arrange the cloves in a single layer and spoon the Chili and Garlic Oil over. Roast, stirring occasionally, until the cloves are lightly browned, 15 to 20 minutes. Watch the garlic as it browns—when it becomes too brown, it takes on a bitter taste.

3.   Cool the garlic and transfer it to a container and refrigerate, covered, until needed.

TO PREPARE AHEAD: Roasted garlic will keep 2 to 3 weeks, refrigerated, in a covered container.

ROASTED WHOLE GARLIC

MAKES ABOUT ¾ CUP

——————————————— ☀ ———————————————

4 whole heads of garlic
(about ¾ pound), unpeeled

About ⅓ cup extra-virgin olive oil

1.   Preheat the oven to 375°F.

2.   Arrange the garlic heads in a small roasting pan and toss with the olive oil, coating them well.

3.   Roast until the garlic is very tender, 50 to 60 minutes. Remove from the oven and cool. When cool, cut the heads in half, crosswise, with a serrated knife and remove the softened garlic pulp. This can be done by squeezing each half or by scooping the garlic out with a tiny teaspoon or small knife.

4.   Transfer to a container, cover, and refrigerate. Use as needed.

TO PREPARE AHEAD: Through step 4.

SAUTÉED ARTICHOKE BOTTOMS

Artichoke bottoms are a real delicacy, the "prize" after all the outer leaves are
peeled away. Not only can you scatter the sliced bottoms over pizza,
but they are especially good tossed with your favorite pasta.

MAKES ENOUGH FOR 2 SMALL PIZZAS

2 large artichokes, about 1 pound each

1 lemon, cut in half

2 tablespoons extra-virgin olive oil

Kosher salt and freshly ground black
pepper

3/4 cup homemade Chicken Stock
(see page 4) or store-bought

1.   Prepare the artichokes: Cut or break off each of the stems, leaving a flat base.
Turn the artichokes with a paring knife, discarding all the leaves, stopping when you
get to the indentation near the bottom of the artichoke. Cut across the indentation
and scoop out the hairy choke with a small teaspoon. Trim around the bottom,
smoothing out the rough edges, and rub with the lemon halves to prevent discol-
oration. Cut each bottom into 6 or 8 wedges and reserve with the lemon halves in
cold water to cover.

2.   When ready to cook, remove the sliced artichokes from the water and drain
well. Heat the oil in a small skillet or sauté pan, add the artichokes, season lightly
with salt and pepper, and sauté over medium heat until lightly golden, 3 to 4 minutes. Pour in the stock and simmer until the artichokes are tender and most of the
liquid has evaporated, about 10 minutes. Adjust the seasoning and use as needed.

TO PREPARE AHEAD: Through step 1 or 2, can be done early in the day and refrigerated,
covered.

DILL CREAM

This tasty cream is spread over the cooked pizza dough before arranging slices of smoked salmon for my signature Smoked Salmon Pizza (see page 86). You can probably find other uses for the cream—say, with savory crepes or potato pancakes.

MAKES ABOUT 1¾ CUPS

1½ cups sour cream

3 tablespoons minced shallots

2 tablespoons chopped fresh dill leaves

1½ tablespoons fresh lemon juice

¼ teaspoon freshly ground white pepper

In a medium bowl, combine all the ingredients and mix well. Refrigerate, covered, and use as needed. This should keep well for up to 1 week.

SALADS

AND SOUPS

CAESAR SALAD WITH HOMEMADE TAPENADE CROUTONS

If you don't have a Caesar salad on your menu in California, the customers will rebel. For a zesty Provençal touch, the Caesar at Spago is served with croutons slathered with our homemade olive tapenade.

When you can find baby romaine, use it. If you can't, trim the outer leaves of the larger variety and, if necessary, break them into bite-size strips.

SERVES 2 TO 4

CROUTONS

1/3 cup olive oil

2 tablespoons freshly grated Parmesan cheese

2 tablespoons minced garlic

1 teaspoon chopped fresh oregano leaves

1 teaspoon chopped fresh thyme leaves

One 1-pound loaf of day-old bread, preferably sourdough, sliced and cut into large cubes (about 2 cups)

1 recipe Black and Green Olive Tapenade (see page 22)

SALAD

2 heads of baby romaine lettuce, or 1 large head of romaine

1 recipe Caesar Vinaigrette (see page 24)

Freshly grated Parmesan cheese, optional

1. Preheat the oven to 350°F.

2. Make the croutons: In a medium bowl, combine the oil, cheese, garlic, oregano, and thyme. Add the bread and toss, coating all the croutons.

3. Arrange the croutons in a single layer on a baking tray and bake until golden, turning to brown all sides. Cool and store in a cool, dry place.

4. Make the salad: Trim the lettuce and toss with some of the Caesar Vinaigrette. Arrange on salad plates and sprinkle with a little Parmesan cheese, if desired.

5.   Spread one side of the croutons with a thin layer of the Black and Green Olive Tapenade. Arrange atop the salads and serve immediately.

TO PREPARE AHEAD: Through step 2, the croutons can be made and will keep for up to 2 weeks in a covered container.

Putting the finishing touch on a feast for stars.

EGGPLANT TOMATO STACK

At the cafés, we offer this as a main-dish salad. However, as an appetizer, two of the wedges will be quite substantial, so select your entrée accordingly. Try to have the eggplant and tomato rounds the same size. If the tomatoes are medium size, buy 2 medium eggplants.

MAKES 2 STACKS; SERVES 2 TO 4

※

1/2 cup extra-virgin olive oil

3 garlic cloves, peeled and crushed

2 sprigs fresh thyme

1 large eggplant (14 to 16 ounces), trimmed and cut into six 1/2-inch round slices

Kosher salt and freshly ground black pepper

1 teaspoon balsamic vinegar

1 large tomato, trimmed and cut into four 1/4-inch slices

3 ounces goat cheese, cut into 4 round slices

2 tablespoons chiffonade of fresh basil leaves

2 cups of arugula, trimmed, washed, and thoroughly dried

About 1/4 cup Spago House Dressing (see page 18)

2 to 3 tablespoons Balsamic Reduction (see page 21)

1.   In a large sauté pan, heat 3 to 4 tablespoons of the olive oil, then add the garlic and thyme, and brown both sides of the eggplant, adding more oil as necessary. Season with salt and pepper. Drain on paper towels and set aside to cool.

2.   Drizzle 2 to 3 tablespoons of the olive oil and the balsamic vinegar over the sliced tomatoes. Season with salt and pepper. Reserve.

3.   Make the stacks: Place one of the eggplant rounds on a firm surface. Top with a slice of tomato; a round of cheese, spreading to cover the tomato; and a sprinkling of the basil chiffonade. Add a second slice of eggplant, tomato, and cheese, more basil, and a last slice of eggplant. Repeat the procedure with the remaining eggplant, tomato, cheese, and basil. Refrigerate until needed.

4. When ready to serve, cut each stack: Cut across one way and then across in the other direction, giving you 4 equal wedges. Season the arugula with salt and pepper to taste and toss with the Spago House Dressing.

5. To serve, divide the arugula and mound in the center of the salad plates. Arrange 2 or 4 wedges around the greens, the points facing out. Drizzle the wedges and around the plates with the Balsamic Reduction and the remaining 1 to 2 table-spoons of olive oil. Serve immediately.

TO PREPARE AHEAD: Through step 2. The stacks can be made about 1 hour before serving.

The Grilled Ahi Tuna Niçoise Salad can be served every season of the year, as long as the tuna is fresh and the vegetables are crisp.

GRILLED AHI TUNA NIÇOISE SALAD

SERVES 2

✳

4 ounces haricots verts

6 tablespoons extra-virgin olive oil

Kosher salt

Freshly ground black pepper

Fresh thyme leaves, minced

1 medium onion, peeled and trimmed

1 each red and yellow bell peppers, roasted, peeled, cored, seeded, trimmed, and cut into ¼-inch strips

¾ cup Niçoise Salad Dressing (see page 45)

6 ounces fingerling potatoes, boiled and peeled

1 cup red and yellow pear and Sweet 100 cherry tomatoes, cut in halves

2 slices bread, preferably sourdough

½ garlic clove, peeled

2 tablespoons Herbed Goat Cheese (see page 26)

2 teaspoons Black and Green Olive Tapenade (see page 22)

Two 6-ounce center-cut Ahi tuna fillets, seasoned with freshly cracked coriander seeds, cracked black pepper, and kosher salt to taste

4 cups mixed baby lettuces, washed and dried

6 tablespoons pitted Niçoise olives

3 quail eggs, boiled, peeled, and halved

6 anchovy fillets

1.   Trim the haricots verts, then blanch in boiling water and refresh in cold water. Drain and season with 1 tablespoon olive oil, salt, pepper, and thyme to taste. Reserve in a bowl.

2.   Cut the onion into ¼-inch round slices. In a small sauté pan, heat 2 tablespoons olive oil. Sauté the onions until caramelized, about 10 minutes, stirring constantly. Season with salt and pepper to taste. Reserve in a bowl.

3.   In a small bowl, toss together the roasted peppers and ⅛ cup Niçoise Salad Dressing. Reserve.

4. Cut the potatoes into ¼-inch round slices. Place in a small bowl, add ¼ cup Niçoise Salad Dressing, and toss until well blended. Reserve.

5. In a small bowl, toss together the tomatoes and ⅛ cup Niçoise Salad Dressing. Reserve.

6. To make crostini: Arrange the bread slices in a baking tray. Brush with olive oil and bake in a preheated 350°F oven for 6 to 8 minutes. Allow to cool, then rub with garlic clove. For each of the crostini, spread 1 tablespoon Herbed Goat Cheese and top with 1 teaspoon Black and Green Olive Tapenade.

7. In a small saucepan, over high heat, add the remaining 2 to 2½ tablespoons olive oil and sear tuna fillets until all sides are brown, about 1 to 2 minutes, keeping the centers rare. Remove from heat and slice each tuna fillet into 5 round slices.

8. In a medium mixing bowl, toss together the mixed baby lettuces with ¼ cup Niçoise Salad Dressing.

9. To serve, divide the haricots verts, onion, bell peppers, potatoes, tomatoes, and olives into 6 portions. For each plate, arrange 3 portions of each ingredient by placing them in a clockwise fashion, starting with the haricots verts at 1, 5, and 9 o'clock positions near the rim of the plate. Continue to place the onion, bell peppers, potatoes, tomatoes, and olives between the haricots verts. Place quail egg halves over the peppers and an anchovy over the potatoes. Mound half of the lettuce in the center of each plate. Arrange the tuna slices on the side of the salad and top the lettuce with the crostini.

NIÇOISE SALAD DRESSING

MAKES 2½ CUPS

¼ cup fresh lemon juice

¼ cup red wine vinegar

¼ cup Dijon mustard

2 tablespoons minced garlic

2 tablespoons minced shallots

1½ cups extra-virgin olive oil

Kosher salt

Freshly ground white pepper

Sugar

In a medium bowl, whisk together lemon juice, vinegar, mustard, garlic, and shallots. Slowly whisk in the olive oil to emulsify. Season to taste with salt, pepper, and sugar. Refrigerate in a covered container. When ready to use, whisk again.

TO PREPARE AHEAD: Dressing will keep up to 2 weeks, refrigerated, in a covered container.

SPINACH AND BLUE CHEESE SALAD WITH SLICED APPLES AND SPICED CARAMELIZED PECANS

Make the salad with baby spinach if it is available. If the spinach leaves are large, break them into smaller pieces. The apple should be tart and crisp. A firm pear can be substituted for the apple, if desired.

SERVES 4

❋

1 apple, chilled

Juice of 1 small lemon

8 ounces spinach, washed, thoroughly dried, and stemmed

1 small head of radicchio (about 3 ounces), cut into chiffonade

5 ounces blue cheese, crumbled

Kosher salt and freshly ground white pepper

About 1/2 cup Spago House Dressing (see page 18)

1 1/2 cups Spiced Caramelized Pecans (see page 25)

1. Cut the apple into quarters, remove the stem and the seeds, and cut into very thin slices. Sprinkle lemon juice over the slices and set aside.

2. When ready to serve, in a salad bowl, combine the apple, spinach, radicchio, and blue cheese. Season lightly with salt and pepper and toss with the dressing. Adjust seasoning to taste.

3. To serve, divide the salad among 4 plates and sprinkle the pecans around each salad.

TO PREPARE AHEAD: All the ingredients can be prepared early in the day. Refrigerate everything but the pecans. Assemble the salad when ready to serve.

ROASTED BEET NAPOLEON

This stacked salad has become a standard at Spago. Rounds of brilliant red beets layered with slices of white goat cheese make up one of the most striking and elegant appetizers we serve. The earthy beets and pungent cheese ask for just a drizzle of House Dressing and a sprinkling of toasted nuts. Add some greens for more color, or serve it without. Easy to make, this is the appetizer for impressing your friends.

Try to purchase beets that are all about the same size. To save time, roast and chill the beets beforehand.

SERVES 2

1½ pounds large yellow or red beets, washed and trimmed

½ cup rice wine vinegar*

½ cup granulated sugar

1 tablespoon extra-virgin olive oil

½ recipe Herbed Goat Cheese (see page 26), cut into eight round slices

1 to 1½ cups mixed baby lettuces, washed and dried

¼ cup Spago House Dressing (see page 18)

¼ cup Citrus Hazelnut Vinaigrette (see page 50)

1 ounce toasted hazelnuts (see page 10), coarsely chopped

1.   Roast beets: Preheat oven to 400°F. Place the beets in a small roasting pan and pour in enough cold water to reach about one quarter of the way up the sides of the beets. Cover the pan with foil, and roast the beets until they are tender, 2 hours to 2 hours and 15 minutes. To check for doneness, gently insert a bamboo skewer into a beet. The skewer should slide through easily. Remove the beets from the pan, allow to cool, and then peel.

2.   Cut each beet into ¼-inch-thick round slices. Cut each slice with a 3-inch round cookie cutter. (You will need ten rounds.) Cut trimmings into ¼-inch dice and reserve ½ cup for garnish.

*Rice wine vinegar is available at Asian markets and gourmet specialty stores.

3.   In a sauté pan, bring vinegar and sugar to a boil. Lower to a simmer and poach beets one minute on each side. With a slotted spatula, remove and place on a baking tray lined with parchment paper. Cover and refrigerate until needed.

4.   When ready to assemble, heat the olive oil in a small sauté pan. Arrange the slices of Herbed Goat Cheese in the pan and warm slightly, turning them with a small spatula just to warm both sides. This has to be done quickly or the cheese will melt.

5.   To assemble the napoleons: Place one of the beet rounds on a firm, flat surface and begin to layer. Top with a slice of goat cheese, then another beet round, a second slice of cheese, another beet round, a third slice of cheese and a beet round. (Continue until you have five layers of beets and four layers of cheese.) Carefully cut through layers, dividing into three wedges. Repeat with the remaining beets and cheese.

6.   To serve: Arrange three of the wedges, pointed ends facing out, in a circle in the center of each plate. Toss the baby lettuces with the Spago House Dressing and mound half of the lettuces on top of each arranged napoleon. Drizzle one half of the Citrus Hazelnut Vinaigrette around each mound. Sprinkle toasted nuts and reserved diced beets on top of drizzled vinaigrette. Serve immediately.

TO PREPARE AHEAD: Through step 3, up to one day ahead.

Roasted Beet Napoleon is a colorful stack of sliced beets sandwiched with fresh goat cheese. Customers rebel if we take it off the menu.

CITRUS HAZELNUT VINAIGRETTE

MAKES 1⅓ CUPS

1½ cups fresh orange juice

1 shallot, peeled and minced

1 teaspoon minced fresh thyme leaves

2 tablespoons balsamic vinegar

½ teaspoon orange zest

⅓ cup hazelnut oil

⅓ cup extra-virgin olive oil

Kosher salt

Freshly ground black pepper

1. In a medium saucepan, bring orange juice to a boil. Lower to a simmer and reduce until only ⅓ cup remains. Cool to room temperature.

2. In a medium bowl, combine orange juice, shallots, thyme, vinegar, and orange zest.

3. Slowly whisk in both oils until thick and emulsified. Season with salt and pepper. Refrigerate until needed.

TO PREPARE AHEAD: The vinaigrette will keep up to 1 week, refrigerated, in a covered container.

GREEK SHRIMP SALAD

With the addition of shrimp, this salad goes from the ordinary Greek salad to the extraordinary Greek salad. Now it has all the elements of the Mediterranean from both sea and land. Add some love and it's even better!

SERVES 4

SHRIMP DRESSING

¹⁄₂ cup plain yogurt

2 tablespoons fresh lemon juice

2 tablespoons cucumber, peeled, seeded, and finely diced

1 tablespoon minced red onion

1 tablespoon minced fresh dill leaves

1 teaspoon minced garlic

Pinch of cayenne pepper

Kosher salt

Freshly ground black pepper

SALAD

1 romaine heart, torn into bite-size pieces

4 cups mixed baby lettuces, washed and dried

¹⁄₂ cup each red and yellow bell peppers, cored, seeded, trimmed, and cut into 1-inch cubes

¹⁄₂ cup Caramelized Onions (see page 28)

¹⁄₂ cup Kalamata olives, pitted

1 small cucumber, peeled, seeded, quartered, cut into ¹⁄₂-inch slices

1 cup yellow pear and Sweet 100 cherry tomatoes, cut in halves

¹⁄₂ cup freshly grated Parmesan cheese

1 cup crumbled feta cheese

1 cup Greek Salad Dressing (see page 52)

Kosher salt

Freshly ground black pepper

16 large shrimp, peeled, deveined, cut in half horizontally, blanched

¹⁄₄ cup toasted pine nuts*

Sprigs of fresh dill

---

*To toast pine nuts, place the nuts in a small skillet in a single layer. Over low heat, toast until lightly golden, stirring often to prevent burning. This takes 3 or 4 minutes. Drain on paper towels.

1.   Make the Shrimp Dressing: In a medium bowl, whisk together the first six ingredients until well blended. Season with cayenne, salt, and pepper to taste. Refrigerate in a covered container. When ready to use, whisk again.

2.   In a large mixing bowl, combine the romaine, baby lettuces, bell peppers, onions, olives, cucumber, tomatoes, cheeses, and Greek Salad Dressing. Toss until blended. Season with salt and pepper. Divide and mound onto 4 chilled salad plates.

3.   In a medium bowl, toss together the shrimp and Shrimp Dressing. Arrange 8 shrimp halves over and around salad mound. Top with pine nuts and garnish with dill sprigs.

GREEK SALAD DRESSING

MAKES 2½ CUPS

1 tablespoon minced fresh dill leaves

1 tablespoon minced fresh parsley leaves

1 tablespoon minced fresh thyme leaves

1 cup plain yogurt

2 tablespoons minced garlic

¼ cup Dijon mustard

¼ cup red wine vinegar

⅓ cup fresh lemon juice

½ teaspoon kosher salt

¼ teaspoon freshly ground white pepper

1½ cups extra-virgin olive oil

Sugar

In a medium bowl, whisk together the dill, parsley, thyme, yogurt, garlic, mustard, vinegar, lemon juice, salt, and pepper. Slowly whisk in the oil, and when emulsified, season with sugar to taste. Refrigerate in a covered container. When ready to use, whisk again.

TO PREPARE AHEAD: Dressing will keep 2 weeks, refrigerated, in a covered container.

GAZPACHO

If you don't want to serve a salad, this is the perfect first course on a warm summer evening, when tomatoes are bursting with flavor. It requires no cooking and can be made the day before it is needed. If the texture is too thick for your taste, stir in a little tomato juice.

MAKES 3 QUARTS

10 (about 2 pounds) Roma tomatoes, cored and chopped

1/2 red bell pepper, cored, seeded, and chopped

1 English cucumber, peeled, seeded, and chopped

2 medium celery stalks, chopped

1/2 cup fresh flat-leaf parsley leaves

1 tablespoon tomato paste

2 cups tomato juice

1/2 cup water

1/4 cup sherry wine vinegar

1 cup extra-virgin olive oil

3 tablespoons sugar

2 tablespoons kosher salt

1/2 teaspoon freshly ground black pepper

1/2 to 1 teaspoon cayenne pepper

1 teaspoon sweet paprika

TOPPING MIXTURE

1/4 cup red bell pepper, cored, seeded, trimmed, and cut into 1/4-inch dice

1/4 cup yellow bell pepper, cored, seeded, trimmed, and cut into 1/4-inch dice

1/4 cup red onion, peeled, trimmed, and cut into 1/4-inch dice

1/4 cup cucumber, peeled, seeded, and cut into 1/4-inch dice

1/2 cup red and yellow pear tomatoes, coarsely chopped

3 ripe avocados, peeled, seeded, and cut into 1/2-inch dice

1 cup minced fresh cilantro leaves

1/4 cup fresh lime juice

Kosher salt

Freshly ground black pepper

12 to 16 large shrimp, peeled, deveined, butterflied, poached, and chilled

6 to 8 sprigs of fresh cilantro

6 to 8 wedges of lime

1. Prepare Gazpacho: In a large bowl, combine all the ingredients. Cover and refrigerate for 1 hour.

2. Transfer to a food processor, pulse until almost puréed, leaving a little texture. Season with salt and pepper. Return to bowl, cover, and refrigerate another hour before serving.

3. Prepare topping mixture: In a medium bowl, combine all the ingredients until well blended. Season with salt and pepper. Cover and refrigerate until needed.

4. To serve: Ladle 10 to 12 ounces into chilled soup plates. On a large serving spoon, place ¼ cup of the topping mixture, top with 2 shrimp, and garnish with a sprig of cilantro. Carefully place in the center of the plate of soup. Place a wedge of lime on the rim of the plate.

TO PREPARE AHEAD: Through step 2. Soup can be prepared up to 2 days ahead before serving. Keep refrigerated.

CREAMY CAULIFLOWER SOUP

MAKES 3 QUARTS

2 large heads cauliflower (about 5 pounds), trimmed and washed

2 tablespoons unsalted butter

¼ cup extra-virgin olive oil, plus more for serving

1 yellow onion (about ½ pound), peeled, trimmed, and sliced

3 garlic cloves, peeled and chopped

Kosher salt

1 medium tomato (about ½ pound), blanched, peeled, seeded, and diced

1½ teaspoons ground cumin

Pinch of sugar

Freshly ground white pepper

1 bay leaf

2 to 3 sprigs of fresh thyme

2 quarts homemade Chicken Stock (see page 4) or Vegetable Stock (see page 6) or store-bought

1 cup heavy cream

Chopped fresh chives, for garnish

1. Cut the heads of cauliflower into thin slices and set aside.

2. In a medium stockpot, melt the butter with the olive oil. Add the onion and garlic and sauté over low heat until translucent. Add the cauliflower and stir to combine with the onion and garlic. Season lightly with salt and cover the pot.

3. Over low heat, cook, stirring often, until the cauliflower is *completely* tender, almost mushy, about 1 hour. Stir in the diced tomato, cumin, sugar, pepper, bay leaf, thyme, and stock. When the soup comes to a boil, pour in the cream. When the soup comes to a boil again, remove it from the heat and discard the bay leaf and thyme.

4. Purée the soup in a food processor in batches, using the pulse button. While the soup is still hot, check and adjust the seasoning to taste.

5. To serve, reheat the soup over low heat and spoon into warm bowls. Drizzle a little olive oil over the soup and sprinkle with chopped chives. Serve immediately.

Served with a few crackers and a good glass of wine, this dramatically presented Savory Squash Soup is a meal in itself.

SAVORY SQUASH SOUP

Fall and winter squash have a long season and are easily stored for months on end. Because our customers love it so much, we have this soup on the menu at Spago six months out of the year. The ginger and cardamom enhance the sweetness of the squash and add an exotic note. The soup can be served warm or cold. For the vegetarian, the soup can be made with a vegetable stock.

MAKES 2 QUARTS

2 butternut squash (about 3¾ pounds)

1 acorn squash (about 1¾ pounds)

6 tablespoons (¾ stick) unsalted butter

1 white onion (about 4 ounces), peeled, trimmed, and finely diced

½ teaspoon kosher salt

⅛ teaspoon freshly ground white pepper

¼ teaspoon ground nutmeg

¼ teaspoon ground ginger

⅛ teaspoon ground cardamom

4 cups homemade Chicken Stock (see page 4) or Vegetable Stock (see page 6) or store-bought, heated

1 cup heavy cream

1 sprig of fresh rosemary

GARNISH

1 recipe Cranberry Relish (see page 58)

1 recipe Cardamom Cream (see page 59)

½ recipe Spiced Caramelized Pecans (see page 25)

4 tablespoons pumpkin seed oil

1. Preheat the oven to 350°F.

2. Cut each squash in half and discard the seeds. Brush cut sides with 2 tablespoons of melted butter. Season with salt, pepper, and nutmeg. Arrange the squash cut side down on a rack placed in a baking tray and bake until tender, about 1½ hours. Cool, scoop out the insides of the squash, and purée the flesh in a food processor. Reserve. (You should have about 4 cups of puréed squash.)

3.   In a medium stockpot, melt the remaining 4 tablespoons of butter. Over low heat, sweat the onion. Do not allow it to brown. Add the puréed squash and cook over very low heat until heated through, stirring occasionally. Do not allow it to bubble up. Season with the salt, pepper, ginger, and cardamom.

4.   Pour in the stock and bring to a boil, still over low heat, stirring often. Cook about 20 minutes.

5.   In a small saucepan, heat the cream with the rosemary sprig. Remove the rosemary and pour the cream into the soup. Transfer to a blender or food processor and process, in batches, for 2 or 3 minutes. Adjust the seasoning to taste.

6.   To serve, ladle the soup into heated bowls. Place a tablespoon of Cranberry Relish in the center, top with a dollop of Cardamom Cream, then sprinkle with chopped pecans. Drizzle pumpkin seed oil over soup.

NOTE: If desired, bake small squash until tender, scoop out, and use as individual serving bowls.

TO PREPARE AHEAD: Through step 5, reheating over low heat.

CRANBERRY RELISH

MAKES 1⅓ CUPS

2 cups fresh cranberries

½ cup sugar

½ cup verjus or 3 tablespoons lemon juice

In a small saucepan, combine all the ingredients. Bring to a boil, then lower to a simmer. Continue to cook until the mixture is thick and the berries are glazed. Allow to cool. Transfer to a covered container and refrigerate until needed.

TO PREPARE AHEAD: Relish will keep up to 2 weeks, refrigerated.

CARDAMOM CREAM

2 cups heavy cream   *1 tablespoon black cardamom seeds*

1.   In a small saucepan, bring 1 cup of heavy cream and the cardamom to a boil. Reduce until only ¼ cup remains. Allow to cool. Reserve.

2.   Whip the remaining 1 cup of heavy cream until stiff peaks form. Stir in the reserved mixture. Chill until ready to serve.

The larger-than-life Oscar statues in front of the Shrine Auditorium.

TORTILLA SOUP

I fell in love with this soup many years ago when I worked at the Mansion on Turtle Creek in Dallas. Though the flavors are full and robust, its tomato-broth base keeps it light and delicate. This soup exemplifies the subtle complexities of Southwestern cuisine. It has become a standard soup in all of the Wolfgang Puck Cafés.

MAKES 3 QUARTS

2 ears of fresh corn, husks removed

4 or 5 large garlic cloves, peeled

1 small onion (about 3 ounces), peeled, trimmed, and quartered

1 small jalapeño pepper, trimmed and seeded

2 tablespoons corn oil

2 corn tortillas, cut into 1-inch squares

2 large ripe tomatoes (1 pound), peeled, seeded, and coarsely chopped

2 tablespoons tomato paste

2 to 3 teaspoons ground cumin

2 quarts homemade Chicken Stock (see page 4) or store-bought, heated

Kosher salt and freshly ground black pepper

GARNISH

2 corn tortillas

1 ripe avocado

1 large chicken breast, cooked, boned, and skinned

½ cup grated Cheddar cheese

¼ cup chopped fresh cilantro leaves

1.   Using a large knife, carefully scrape the kernels off the corn cobs and set aside, reserving the cobs.

2.   Using a food processor fitted with the steel blade, or a large knife, coarsely chop the garlic, onion, jalapeño pepper, and the corn kernels. Reserve.

3.   Make the soup: In a large soup pot, heat the oil. Add the squares of tortillas and cook over low heat until they are slightly crisp. Stir in the chopped vegetables and simmer just until the vegetables are coated with the oil. Do not brown.

4.   Add the tomatoes, the tomato paste, and 2 teaspoons of the cumin and continue to simmer for about 10 minutes to maximize the flavor. Slowly pour in the stock, add the corn cobs, and cook over low heat until the soup is reduced by one third.

5.   Discard the corn cobs and purée the soup, in batches, in a blender or food processor until smooth. At this point, the soup can be passed through a fine strainer if desired. Return to a clean pot and season with salt, pepper, and additional cumin to taste.

6.   Prepare the garnish: Preheat the oven or toaster oven to 350°F. Cut the tortillas into thin strips and arrange on a small baking tray. Bake until the strips are crisp, 10 to 15 minutes. Peel and dice the avocado. Cut the chicken into thin strips.

7.   To serve, add the chicken and avocado to the soup and reheat over low heat. Ladle the soup into 6 to 8 warm soup bowls and garnish with the baked tortilla strips, Cheddar cheese, and chopped cilantro. Serve immediately.

TO PREPARE AHEAD: Through step 5, the soup can be made early in the day. The tortilla strips for the garnish can be crisped early in the day as well. The chicken should be sliced and the avocado diced just before adding to the soup.

WHITE BEAN SOUP

This is perfect for a cool winter evening. The bacon does give the soup a distinct flavor, but it can be eliminated if desired.

MAKES 3 QUARTS

───────────── ☀ ─────────────

2 cups dry white beans

¼ cup extra-virgin olive oil

2 ounces smoked bacon (about 3 slices) cut into strips

2 medium onions (1 pound), peeled, trimmed, and diced

2 large carrots, trimmed, peeled, and diced (¾ cup)

2 small celery stalks, trimmed and diced (½ cup)

1 small celery root, peeled and diced

6 garlic cloves, peeled and chopped

¼ cup tomato paste

1 large tomato (8 ounces), peeled, seeded, and chopped

2 or 3 fresh basil leaves

2 or 3 sprigs of fresh flat-leaf parsley

1 sprig of fresh thyme

1 sprig of fresh rosemary

⅓ cup sherry wine vinegar

2 teaspoons sugar

2½ quarts homemade Chicken Stock (see page 4) or Vegetable Stock (see page 6) or store-bought, heated

Kosher salt and freshly ground white pepper

Sliced cooked sausage, for garnish, optional

Braised Swiss chard, for garnish, optional

Freshly grated Parmesan cheese, for garnish, optional

1.   In a large bowl, soak the beans overnight in cold water to cover. Drain.

2.   Heat a large stockpot and pour in the olive oil. Add the strips of bacon and cook for a few minutes to render flavor to the soup. Remove the bacon.

3.   Add the onions, carrots, celery, and celery root and cook over medium heat, stirring occasionally, until just tender, 3 to 4 minutes.

4.   Stir in the garlic, tomato paste, chopped tomato, and the drained beans. Tie together the basil, parsley, thyme, and rosemary. Add to the pot with the vinegar and the sugar. Pour in the stock and stir to combine thoroughly. Season lightly with salt and pepper.

5.   Cook over medium heat until the beans are tender, 2 to 2½ hours, stirring occasionally, adding more stock as necessary.

6.   Discard the herbs. Remove 2 cups of the beans and vegetables and purée in a blender or food processor. Stir the purée back into the soup and adjust the seasoning to taste.

7.   To serve, spoon the soup into heated bowls. Garnish with sausage, Swiss chard, or Parmesan cheese, if desired.

CHICKEN BOUILLON WITH CHICKEN, HERB CREPES, AND JULIENNE OF VEGETABLES

MAKES 4 TO 5 QUARTS

BOUILLON

1/4 cup extra-virgin olive oil

2 medium onions, peeled, trimmed, and thinly sliced

2 medium carrots, peeled, trimmed, and cut into 1/2-inch pieces

2 large celery stalks, trimmed and cut into 1-inch pieces

1 large leek, cut in half lengthwise, washed, trimmed, and cut into 1-inch pieces

1 large parsnip, peeled, trimmed, and cut into 1/2-inch pieces

1/2 cup garlic cloves, peeled and chopped

1/2 cup shallots, peeled, trimmed, and thinly sliced

1/2 bunch fresh parsley

5 sprigs fresh thyme

2 bay leaves

5 whole cloves, crushed

1 teaspoon whole black peppercorns

1 whole chicken (3 to 4 pounds), wrapped in cheesecloth

5 to 6 quarts (or enough to cover chicken) Chicken Stock (see page 4) or store-bought

2 to 3 tablespoons kosher salt

Freshly ground white pepper

2 to 3 tablespoons sugar

GARNISH

1 cup each of julienne of carrots, leeks, and celery root (or celery)

1 recipe Herb Crepes (see page 65), trim all sides to form a square and cut into 1/4-inch strips

2 cups (about 12 ounces) bone marrow, cut into 1/2-inch slices, optional

1/4 cup minced fresh chives

1. In a 12-quart stockpot, heat the olive oil over high heat. Sauté the onions, carrots, celery, leeks, parsnips, garlic, and shallots until soft. Do not brown.

2. Make a sachet: Combine the parsley, thyme, bay leaves, cloves, and pepper-corns. Wrap them in cheesecloth, tie the bundle with kitchen twine, and add it to the stockpot.

3. Add the chicken, chicken stock, salt, and sugar. Bring to a boil, and skim off any foam that rises to the top. Lower to a simmer and cook for 2 hours.

4. Remove the chicken, and when it's cool to the touch, unwrap it. Discard the skin and remove the meat from the bones. Shred the chicken into ¼-inch by 2-inch strips. Reserve, covered, in the refrigerator until ready to use.

5. Pass the bouillon through a chinois or fine strainer. Season with the salt, pepper, and sugar.

6. To serve, reheat the bouillon, add the reserved chicken strips and julienne of vegetables, and simmer for 1 minute. Add the crepes and bone marrow and simmer for 1 minute. Ladle about 1½ cups into soup bowls and garnish with chives. Serve immediately.

TO PREPARE AHEAD: Through step 5. Bouillon can be refrigerated up to 3 to 4 days. When ready to serve, reheat bouillon and continue with step 6.

HERB CREPES

MAKES ABOUT 6 CUPS BATTER (FOR 24 9-INCH CREPES)

3 cups milk

⅔ cup heavy cream

1⅓ cups all-purpose flour

¼ cup minced fresh chervil leaves

¼ cup minced fresh parsley leaves

¼ cup minced fresh chives

4 eggs, room temperature

2 tablespoons melted, clarified, unsalted butter

1 teaspoon kosher salt

Freshly ground white pepper

1.   Make the crepe batter: In a food processor, place all the ingredients and process until well blended. Transfer to a medium-size bowl, cover, and refrigerate for at least one hour.

2.   Make Herb Crepes: Heat a 10½-inch nonstick sauté pan over medium heat. Pour in 1½ ounces of batter and spread it to cover the bottom of the pan. Cook the crepe until its top begins to dry and its bottom is golden brown. Turn to brown the other side, then remove from pan. Repeat until all the batter is gone.

3.   Stack the cooled crepes and cover. Refrigerate until ready to use.

TO PREPARE AHEAD: Crepes can be refrigerated for 4 to 5 days or frozen for up to a week. (To prevent them from tearing during the thawing process, place crepes between sheets of parchment paper.)

A chef never eats—he tastes.

PIZZA

Pizza is the friendliest food I know of. It's hard for people to say no to a slice, especially when it's topped with flavorful, fresh ingredients. If you don't believe me, serve a large group of friends some pizza, then stand back and watch them eat! From small children, finicky teenagers, and the most sophisticated diners, pizza always evokes a smile. Its simplicity and versatility make it appealing to everyone. I had my first pizza in the south of France. I'll never forget my sense of amazement and satisfaction as I sampled that crisp, thin crust topped with just the right proportion of tomato sauce and cheese. A late-night visit to the local café for pizza quickly became a habit. Years later, when I was living in Los Angeles, I realized no one was making those tasty pizzas I had eaten in Europe. The big pizza chains served a doughy variety, laden with canned tomato sauce and greasy processed meats. Why wasn't anyone making real pizza in southern California?

When we were building the kitchen of the original Spago back in 1981, I discovered the answer. To duplicate that European-style pizza, I would need a wood-fired oven. Only then could I achieve that crisp, delicious crust scented with a deep, smoky flavor. Moreover, the visual drama of an open kitchen with a wood-fired oven would entice the guests and make them feel a part of the process. But getting the permits for this unusual restaurant "appliance" was not an easy feat. After many phone calls and much perseverance, we finally got the city's okay. The wood-fired oven was built by a German mason, and there began the legend. When the restaurant finally opened, we could barely keep up; pizza was the most frequently ordered item on the menu. It was infectious. When a new party sat down and glanced around at the pizzas on all the other tables or eyed the steaming hot pizzas coming out of the oven, they couldn't resist. Every table had to have one!

With so many unique and amazing ingredients to choose from in California, I developed a multinational approach to the toppings for my pizzas. The Greek pizza has spinach, tomatoes, eggplant, red onion, oregano, and feta cheese with a little pesto spread over the crust—a true Mediterranean feast. The ever-popular Caesar salad found its way onto a pizza, too. And Shrimp and Goat Cheese Pizza has always been a hit. I've included the classic Pepperoni and Mushroom for those who just won't be adventurous. If you don't see your favorite vegetables or ingredients here, improvise! That's the beauty and fun of making your own pizzas at home. Many home cooks are afraid to make their own pizzas. The dough is alive: It changes and goes through different stages. People get scared and don't know what to expect. It always reminds me of the first time I held my firstborn son. I was so nervous and confused; I was sure I was holding him too tightly, or not tightly enough. It took only a couple of times until I felt comfortable and self-assured. It's the same with pizza dough. Kids especially love to make pizzas! They jump right in and love to play with the dough. When my son Cameron invites his friends to our house, that's always the first thing they ask: "Do we get to make pizza?"

Though I love the results of a wood-fired pizza oven, a conventional oven makes delicious pizza, too. Make your dough, let it rise, turn the oven up to 500°F, and you're on your way! Mixing the dough, watching it rise, and rolling and shaping it is just the beginning of this exciting task. Staring into the hot oven as the dough puffs slightly and develops those perfectly browned edges is a pleasure not to be missed. Slide the bubbling hot pizza onto a plate and watch it disappear. To eat it, to make it, and to watch people eating it brings me so much joy!

2.
On a lightly floured surface, stretch the dough into a small circle and begin to knead it by pressing down in the center, leaving the outer edge thicker than the inner circle.

1.
Once you have rolled the piece of dough into a ball, work it with your hands on a smooth surface by pulling down the sides and tucking under the bottom of the ball. Repeat 4 to 5 times. Roll the ball under the palm of your hand until the top of the dough is smooth and firm, about 1 minute.

3.
Pulling and stretching it with both hands, elongate the dough into an oval.

PIZZA DOUGH

You can make four pizzas, as described below, or you can divide the dough in half and make two large 12-inch pizzas. The baking time will be the same.

Chopped fresh basil, chopped sun-dried tomatoes, or a sprinkling of crushed red pepper flakes can be added to the dough with the flour, if desired, for additional flavor. Be creative with your pizzas! For the best results, see "Pizza Tips" on page 75.

MAKES FOUR 8-INCH PIZZAS
(MAKES ABOUT 24 OUNCES OF DOUGH)

1 package active dry or fresh yeast

1 teaspoon honey

1 cup warm water (105°F. to 115°F.)

3 cups all-purpose flour

1 teaspoon kosher salt

1 tablespoon extra-virgin olive oil or Chili and Garlic Oil (see page 20), plus more for brushing

Topping of your choice

1.   In a small bowl, dissolve the yeast and honey in ¼ cup of the warm water.

2.   In a mixer fitted with a dough hook, combine the flour and the salt. Add the oil, your mixture, and the remaining ¾ cup of water and mix on low speed until the dough comes cleanly away from the sides of the bowl and clusters around the dough hook, about 5 minutes. (The pizza dough can also be made in a food processor. Dissolve the yeast as above. Combine the flour and salt in the bowl of a food processor fitted with the steel blade. Pulse once or twice, add the remaining ingredients, and process until the dough begins to form a ball.)

3.   Turn the dough out onto a clean work surface and knead by hand 2 or 3 minutes longer. The dough should be smooth and firm. Cover the dough with a clean, damp towel and let it rise in a warm spot for about 30 minutes. (When ready, the dough will stretch as it is lightly pulled.)

4.   Divide the dough into 4 balls, about 6 ounces each. Work each ball by pulling down the sides and tucking under the bottom of the ball. Repeat 4 or 5 times. Then on a smooth, unfloured surface, roll the ball under the palm of your hand until the top of the dough is smooth and firm, about 1 minute. Cover the dough with a damp towel and let it rest for 15 to 20 minutes. At this point, the balls can be wrapped in plastic and refrigerated for up to 2 days.

5.   Place a pizza stone on the middle rack of the oven and preheat the oven to 500°F.

6.   To prepare each pizza, dip the ball of dough into flour, shake off the excess flour, place the dough on a clean, lightly floured surface, and start to stretch the dough. Press down on the center, spreading the dough into an 8-inch circle, with the outer border a little thicker than the inner circle. If you find this difficult to do, use a small rolling pin to roll out the dough. Lightly brush the inner circle of the dough with oil and arrange the topping of your choice over the inner circle.

7.   Using a lightly floured baker's peel or a rimless flat baking tray, slide the pizza onto the baking stone and bake until the pizza crust is nicely browned, 10 to 12 minutes. Remember that the oven is very hot and be careful as you place the pizza into and out of the oven. Transfer the pizza to a firm surface and cut into slices with a pizza cutter or very sharp knife. Serve immediately.

TO PREPARE AHEAD: Through step 4. When ready to serve, remove the balls of dough from the refrigerator and let them rest at room temperature for about 15 minutes, then continue with the recipe. Through step 7, bake 5 or 6 minutes, until the cheese melts and the pizza dough is lightly golden brown. (At this point, the pizza can be cooled, wrapped well, and frozen for up to 1 month.) When needed, remove from the freezer, unwrap, and bake in a preheated oven until the crust has browned and the topping is heated through.

PIZZA TIPS

1. In step 4, if you wrap the dough in plastic wrap and refrigerate, make certain that you wrap each ball of dough *loosely but completely*. Since you are working with a yeast dough, the dough will expand as it stays in the refrigerator. If it is not wrapped well, the dough will ooze out of its wrapping and harden. You may want to enclose the dough in a resealable plastic bag.

2. Make certain that you stretch or roll out the dough on a floured surface, preferably on a baker's peel, a rimless flat baking tray, or a very wide spatula that you are using to transfer the pizza to the oven.

3. Have all the ingredients ready so that you can arrange them on the pizza dough at serving time. At the restaurants we place the ingredients in separate bowls so that they are easily available when we need them.

4. In order to make the very best pizza possible, you'll need to have a mixer with dough hook (or food processor), a pizza stone, a baker's peel, a rimless baking tray or very wide spatula, and a pizza cutter or large sharp knife.

5. Make certain that the ingredients that have been sautéed are not hot when you arrange them on the pizza. This will soften the dough, and if the dough gets too soft it will be difficult to release it from the peel to the oven. Put the toppings on the pizza dough just before transferring it to the oven.

6. My recipes recommend an oven temperature of 500°F. If your oven thermostat does not reach 500°F., preheat it to the highest possible temperature.

7. Check the pizza after 10 minutes, since every oven bakes differently, and if it is not browned enough, continue to bake 1 or 2 minutes longer.

HERBED ARTICHOKE PIZZA

Most of the time, our philosophy for pizza is "more is more." But, in this case, artichokes, the perfect vegetable, ask for very little. With some Caramelized Onions and chopped fresh herbs, this is the perfect pizza.

MAKES FOUR 8-INCH PIZZAS

* * *

1 recipe Pizza Dough (see page 73)

4 teaspoons Chili and Garlic Oil (see page 20)

1 teaspoon minced fresh thyme leaves

1 teaspoon minced fresh oregano leaves

2 recipes Sautéed Artichoke Bottoms (see page 34)

1 recipe Caramelized Onions (see page 28)

About 4 ounces pitted Niçoise olives

4 teaspoons freshly grated Parmesan cheese

8 large basil leaves, cut into chiffonade, for garnish

1.   Place a pizza stone on the middle rack of the oven and preheat the oven to 500°F. On a lightly floured surface, stretch or roll out each of the balls of dough into an 8-inch circle, the outer edge a little thicker than the inner circle.

2.   Brush each of the circles of dough with the Chili and Garlic Oil. Divide each ingredient into 4 portions.

3.   Layer each of the pizzas: First sprinkle with the thyme and the oregano, then arrange the artichokes, onions, olives, and Parmesan cheese. Bake until the pizza crust is nicely browned, 8 to 10 minutes. Remove them from the oven and garnish with the chiffonade of basil leaves. Transfer the pizzas to a cutting board and cut into slices. Serve immediately.

TO PREPARE AHEAD: Have all the ingredients ready and prepare the pizzas when about to serve.

Herbed Artichoke Pizza, speckled with olives, is as flavorful as it is rustic.

CAMERON'S FOUR-CHEESE PIZZA

When my son Cameron was younger, this was the only pizza he would eat. He told me just what he wanted on *his* pizza, and he's eaten it the same way ever since.

MAKES ONE 10-INCH OR TWO 8-INCH PIZZAS; SERVES 3 TO 4

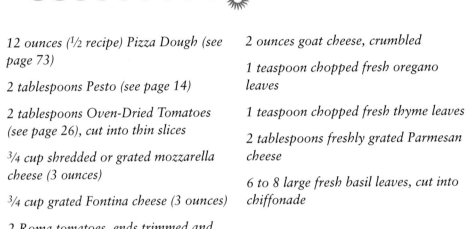

12 ounces (½ recipe) Pizza Dough (see page 73)

2 tablespoons Pesto (see page 14)

2 tablespoons Oven-Dried Tomatoes (see page 26), *cut into thin slices*

¾ cup shredded or grated mozzarella cheese (3 ounces)

¾ cup grated Fontina cheese (3 ounces)

2 Roma tomatoes, ends trimmed and cut into 12 slices

2 ounces goat cheese, crumbled

1 teaspoon chopped fresh oregano leaves

1 teaspoon chopped fresh thyme leaves

2 tablespoons freshly grated Parmesan cheese

6 to 8 large fresh basil leaves, cut into chiffonade

1. Place a pizza stone on the middle rack of the oven and preheat the oven to 500°F.

2. On a lightly floured surface, stretch or roll out the dough into one 10-inch round or two 8-inch rounds. Brush lightly with Pesto and scatter the Oven-Dried Tomatoes evenly around the inner circle of the pizza.

3. Sprinkle with the mozzarella and Fontina cheeses, arrange the slices of the Roma tomatoes, and then sprinkle with the goat cheese, oregano, thyme, and finally the Parmesan cheese. Bake until the pizza crust is nicely browned, 10 to 12 minutes.

4. When the pizza is removed from the oven, transfer to a cutting board and garnish with the chiffonade of basil leaves, cut into slices, and serve immediately.

TO PREPARE AHEAD: Have all the ingredients ready and prepare the pizza when about to serve.

GRILLED PORTABELLA MUSHROOM PIZZA

Portabella mushrooms, which are available a good part of the year, make this a particularly hearty pizza. However, if you prefer, another wild mushroom, such as porcini, shiitake, or black trumpet, can be substituted.

MAKES FOUR 8-INCH PIZZAS OR TWO 12-INCH PIZZAS

1 recipe Pizza Dough (see page 73)

3 tablespoons Chili and Garlic Oil (see page 20)

2 cups grated mozzarella cheese (8 ounces)

2 cups grated Fontina cheese (8 ounces)

1 recipe Caramelized Onions (see page 28)

2 tablespoons sliced Roasted Garlic (see page 32)

2 cups grilled portabella mushrooms, cut into 1/4-inch-thick slices (see Note on next page)

1 tablespoon chopped fresh rosemary leaves

4 ounces goat cheese, cut into small pieces

1/4 cup freshly grated Parmesan cheese

1/4 cup fresh basil leaves, cut into chiffonade, for garnish

1. Place a pizza stone on the middle rack of the oven and preheat the oven to 500°F.

2. On a lightly floured surface, stretch or roll out each piece of dough into an 8-inch round (or two 12-inch rounds).

3. Brush the inner surface of the pizzas with the Chili and Garlic Oil and distribute the toppings, in the order listed, evenly over the inner circles. Bake until the crust is nicely browned, 10 to 12 minutes. Remove from the oven, sprinkle with the basil, and cut into slices. Serve immediately.

TO PREPARE AHEAD: All the ingredients can be prepared ahead. Layer and bake the pizza at serving time.

NOTE: To grill the mushrooms, remove the stems and reserve for stocks. Marinate the mushrooms in a little olive oil, chopped garlic, a pinch of fresh oregano, salt, and freshly ground black pepper. Toss to make certain the mushrooms are well coated. Place the mushrooms on the grill, top sides down first, turning with tongs, and cook until tender to the touch, turning as necessary. Spread on a tray to cool. Do not stack.

If you don't have a grill, cut the mushrooms into thick slices. Heat a little oil in a skillet and sauté the mushrooms, add a little chopped garlic, season as above, and continue to sauté until tender, turning as necessary.

Kitchen notes for the cooks at the Governor's Ball

CAESAR CHICKEN PIZZA

When we had to come up with a signature pizza for the Forum at Caesar's Palace in Las Vegas, this was the obvious choice, of course. Salad on pizza may sound strange, but trust me, after the first bite you'll be hooked. While the lettuce adds a surprising crunchy texture and a contrast of temperatures, the acidity in the dressing complements the tangy chicken. Just like the salad, this pizza never loses its appeal.

MAKES FOUR 8-INCH PIZZAS

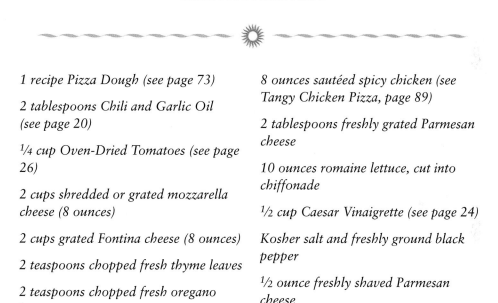

1 recipe Pizza Dough (see page 73)

2 tablespoons Chili and Garlic Oil (see page 20)

¼ cup Oven-Dried Tomatoes (see page 26)

2 cups shredded or grated mozzarella cheese (8 ounces)

2 cups grated Fontina cheese (8 ounces)

2 teaspoons chopped fresh thyme leaves

2 teaspoons chopped fresh oregano leaves

8 ounces sautéed spicy chicken (see Tangy Chicken Pizza, page 89)

2 tablespoons freshly grated Parmesan cheese

10 ounces romaine lettuce, cut into chiffonade

½ cup Caesar Vinaigrette (see page 24)

Kosher salt and freshly ground black pepper

½ ounce freshly shaved Parmesan cheese

1. Place a pizza stone on the middle rack of the oven and preheat the oven to 500°F. On a lightly floured surface, stretch or roll out each of the balls of dough into an 8-inch circle.

2. Brush each of the circles of dough lightly with the Chili and Garlic Oil and start to layer, dividing the ingredients equally among the 4 pizzas. Start with the tomatoes, then the mozzarella and Fontina cheeses, the herbs, chicken, and Parmesan. Bake until the pizza crusts are nicely browned, 10 to 12 minutes.

3.   Toss the lettuce with the vinaigrette and season lightly with salt and pepper. Remove the pizzas from the oven, arrange the lettuce on each of the pizzas, and top with some of the shaved Parmesan. Cut into slices and serve immediately.

TO PREPARE AHEAD: See page 74.

Caesar Chicken Pizza pushes the boundaries of pizza-making. The contrasts of texture and temperature make for a completely new pizza experience.

WHITE CLAM PIZZA

MAKES ONE 8-INCH PIZZA

1 pound steamed Littleneck clams

6 ounces Pizza Dough (see page 73)

1 tablespoon Chili and Garlic Oil (see page 20)

2 tablespoons mascarpone cheese

1/4 cup ricotta cheese

1 teaspoon minced garlic

1/2 teaspoon minced fresh oregano leaves

Pinch of red pepper flakes

1 tablespoon freshly grated Parmesan cheese

1 teaspoon minced flat-leaf fresh parsley leaves

1. Place a pizza stone on the middle rack of the oven and preheat the oven to 500°F.

2. Remove the meat from the steamed clams and reserve. Discard the shells.

3. On a lightly floured surface, stretch or roll out the dough into an 8-inch circle, the outer edge a little thicker than the inner circle. Brush the inner circle with the Chili and Garlic Oil.

4. In a small bowl, combine the mascarpone and ricotta cheeses, the garlic, oregano, and red pepper flakes. Spread over the dough and arrange the reserved clams over the cheese mixture. Sprinkle the Parmesan cheese over the top. Slide the pizza onto the pizza stone and bake until the crust is golden brown, about 6 to 7 minutes.

5. Carefully remove the pizza from the oven and set on a firm surface. Sprinkle the minced parsley over the top. Cut into slices with a pizza cutter or a large sharp chef's knife. Serve immediately.

PROSCIUTTO AND GOAT CHEESE PIZZA

MAKES TWO 8-INCH PIZZAS

12 ounces Pizza Dough (see page 73)

1/4 cup Pesto (see page 14)

1 cup grated mozzarella cheese (4 ounces)

1 cup grated Fontina cheese (4 ounces)

2 Roma tomatoes, ends trimmed and cut into thin slices

2 ounces prosciutto, cut into thin strips

2 ounces goat cheese, cut or crumbled into small pieces

1/4 teaspoon minced fresh oregano leaves

1/4 teaspoon minced fresh thyme leaves

4 teaspoons freshly grated Parmesan cheese

1. Place a pizza stone on the middle rack of the oven and preheat the oven to 500°F.

2. On a lightly floured surface, stretch or roll out each piece of dough into an 8-inch round. For each pizza, brush the round with Pesto and then layer with the mozzarella, Fontina, tomatoes, prosciutto, goat cheese, oregano, thyme, and Parmesan cheese. Bake until the pizza crusts are nicely browned, 10 to 12 minutes. Transfer to a firm surface and cut into slices with a pizza cutter or large sharp knife. Serve immediately.

TO PREPARE AHEAD: All the ingredients can be prepared ahead. Layer and bake the pizza at serving time.

GREEK VEGETABLE PIZZA

This pizza is a Mediterranean treat! Everything you'd find in a Greek salad can be found on this colorful and tasty pizza. Be sure to cook the eggplant until it's nice and tender.

MAKES ONE 8-INCH PIZZA; SERVES 1 OR 2

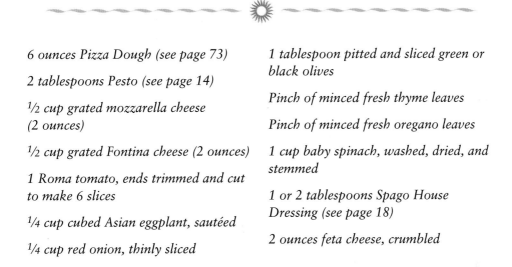

6 ounces Pizza Dough (see page 73)

2 tablespoons Pesto (see page 14)

½ cup grated mozzarella cheese (2 ounces)

½ cup grated Fontina cheese (2 ounces)

1 Roma tomato, ends trimmed and cut to make 6 slices

¼ cup cubed Asian eggplant, sautéed

¼ cup red onion, thinly sliced

1 tablespoon pitted and sliced green or black olives

Pinch of minced fresh thyme leaves

Pinch of minced fresh oregano leaves

1 cup baby spinach, washed, dried, and stemmed

1 or 2 tablespoons Spago House Dressing (see page 18)

2 ounces feta cheese, crumbled

1. Place a pizza stone on the middle rack of the oven and preheat the oven to 500°F.

2. On a lightly floured surface, stretch or roll out the dough into an 8-inch round, the outer edge a little thicker than the inner circle. Brush the inner circle with Pesto and layer with the mozzarella, Fontina, tomato slices, eggplant, red onion, olives, thyme, and oregano.

3. Bake until the crust is nicely browned, 10 to 12 minutes. Remove from the oven and transfer onto a firm surface.

4. Toss the spinach in the dressing and arrange on top of the pizza. Sprinkle the feta cheese over, cut into slices, and serve immediately.

TO PREPARE AHEAD: All the ingredients can be prepared early in the day. Layer and bake the pizza when ready to serve.

SMOKED SALMON PIZZA

When I first opened the original Spago restaurant, this became the signature pizza. Now we don't usually have it on the menu, but all the regular customers know they can always get it at Spago. A glass of champagne is its perfect partner. If you feel decadent you can top the pizza with Sevruga caviar!

MAKES ONE 8-INCH PIZZA

———————————— ✺ ————————————

6 ounces Pizza Dough (see page 73)

1 tablespoon Chili and Garlic Oil (see page 20)

¼ cup thinly sliced red onion

2 tablespoons Dill Cream (see page 35)

2½ ounces thinly sliced smoked salmon

1 teaspoon chopped fresh chives

1 tablespoon Sevruga caviar, optional

1. Place a pizza stone on the middle rack of the oven and preheat the oven to 500°F.

2. On a lightly floured surface, stretch or roll out the dough into an 8-inch circle, with the outer edge a little thicker than the inner circle. Brush the dough with the oil and arrange the onions over the pizza. Bake until the crust is golden brown, 6 to 8 minutes.

3. Carefully remove the pizza from the oven and set on a firm surface. Spread the Dill Cream over the inner circle and arrange the slices of salmon so that they cover the entire pizza, slightly overlapping the inner border. Sprinkle the chopped chives around the top. Using a pizza cutter or a large sharp knife, cut into 4 or 6 slices, and, if you like, spoon a little caviar in the center of each slice. Serve immediately.

TO PREPARE AHEAD: In step 2, bake the pizza for about 5 minutes. At serving time, reheat until browned and continue with the recipe.

TANGY CHICKEN PIZZA

MAKES FOUR 8-INCH PIZZAS

About 1¼ pounds skinned and boned uncooked *chicken, cut into cubes to make 4 cups*

MARINADE

½ cup plus 1 tablespoon extra-virgin olive oil

3½ tablespoons fresh lime juice

2 large jalapeño peppers, trimmed and minced

1 garlic clove, peeled and minced

Pinch of chopped fresh cilantro leaves

Kosher salt

TOPPING

2 cups grated mozzarella cheese (8 ounces)

2 cups grated Fontina cheese (8 ounces)

6 Roma tomatoes (about 1 pound), ends trimmed, cut into thin slices

1 cup cubed Asian eggplant, sautéed or grilled

1 recipe Caramelized Onions (see page 28)

½ cup sliced red and yellow bell peppers, sautéed or grilled

1 recipe Pizza Dough (see page 73)

1.   Marinate the chicken: Arrange the cubed chicken in a shallow medium bowl and toss with the marinade ingredients, using ½ cup of the olive oil. Season lightly with salt and let marinate for about 1 hour, refrigerated.

2.   In a skillet or sauté pan large enough to hold the chicken in one layer, heat the remaining 1 tablespoon of oil. Remove the chicken from the marinade with a slotted spoon. Sauté the chicken just to brown on all sides. Do not overcook. Remove from the skillet with a slotted spoon and set aside.

3.   Place a pizza stone on the middle rack of the oven and preheat the oven to 500°F. On a lightly floured surface, stretch or roll out the dough to make four 8-inch rounds, with the outer edge a little thicker than the inner circle.

4.   Layer the pizza: Start with the mozzarella, then the Fontina, tomato, eggplant, Caramelized Onions, cooked chicken, and peppers. Slide the pizza onto the baking stone. Bake until the pizza is nicely browned, 10 to 12 minutes.

5.   Transfer the pizza to a firm surface and cut into slices with a pizza cutter or very sharp knife. Serve immediately.

TO PREPARE AHEAD: All the ingredients can be prepared early in the day and refrigerated. Assemble the pizzas when ready to serve.

Armies of mini chocolate Oscars get dusted with gold powder. Now *everyone* gets to take home an Oscar.

SPICY SCALLOP AND ARTICHOKE PIZZA

This is *definitely* a spicy topping, not for those who like their food on the milder side. If you've never tasted fresh scallops, then you don't know what you're missing. After that first bite, you'll understand how special they are, sweet and bursting with the essence of the sea. But if you can't find fresh scallops, substitute shrimp or clams.

MAKES FOUR 8-INCH PIZZAS

MARINADE

2 large jalapeño peppers (2 ounces), trimmed, seeded, and minced

3 garlic cloves, peeled and chopped

1 tablespoon plus 1 teaspoon chopped fresh thyme leaves

1/4 cup extra-virgin olive oil

2 cups sea scallops (scant 1 pound), trimmed and cut into quarters

Kosher salt and freshly ground white pepper

1 recipe Pizza Dough (see page 73)

2 tablespoons Chili and Garlic Oil (see page 20)

2 cups grated mozzarella cheese (8 ounces)

2 cups grated Fontina cheese (8 ounces)

4 Roma tomatoes (about 3/4 pound), ends trimmed and cut into thin slices

1 cup sliced cooked artichoke hearts (about 4 ounces)

1 1/3 cups thinly sliced red onion (about 4 ounces)

1/2 cup coarsely chopped fresh cilantro leaves

4 teaspoons freshly grated Parmesan cheese

1.   In a medium bowl, combine the marinade ingredients. Add the scallops and toss to coat well. Season lightly with salt and pepper and refrigerate until needed. When ready to layer the pizzas, remove the scallops with a slotted spoon.

2.   Place a pizza stone on the middle rack of the oven and preheat the oven to 500°F.

3.   On a lightly floured surface, stretch or roll out the dough into four 8-inch rounds, with the outer edge a little thicker than the inner circle. Brush each of the pizza rounds with the Chili and Garlic Oil and begin to layer. First layer with the mozzarella, then the Fontina, tomato, artichoke, and onion. Scatter a little chopped cilantro over the onion, and arrange the scallops over the top. Sprinkle with the remaining cilantro and the grated Parmesan.

4.   Gently slide the pizza onto the baking stone and bake until golden brown, about 10 to 12 minutes.

5.   Transfer the pizza to a firm surface and cut into slices with a pizza cutter or very sharp knife. Serve immediately.

TO PREPARE AHEAD: Through step 1, the scallops can be marinated early in the day.

SPINACH, MUSHROOM, AND BLUE CHEESE PIZZA

When one of my chefs told me about this new pizza he made up, I was a bit nervous and skeptical. Though I use all of these ingredients in other dishes, it sounded odd to me to put them together on a pizza. But once I tried it I was pleasantly surprised. It has turned out to be one of our most popular pizzas. The vegetables do not need to be sautéed in advance but will cook as the pizza bakes in the oven. If you prefer, Gorgonzola cheese can be substituted for blue cheese.

MAKES ONE 8-INCH PIZZA

6 ounces Pizza Dough (see page 73)

2 tablespoons Pesto (see page 14)

1 cup baby spinach leaves, stemmed, washed, and dried

1/2 cup grated mozzarella cheese (2 ounces)

1/2 cup grated Fontina cheese (2 ounces)

1 large Roma tomato, ends trimmed and cut into 7 slices

1/2 cup button mushrooms, stemmed, cleaned, and thinly sliced

1 1/2 ounces blue cheese, crumbled

Pinch of minced fresh oregano leaves

Pinch of minced fresh thyme leaves

1 tablespoon freshly grated Parmesan cheese

1.   Place a pizza stone on the middle rack of the oven and preheat the oven to 500°F.

2.   On a lightly floured surface, stretch or roll the dough into an 8-inch round and brush the inner circle with the Pesto. Arrange the spinach leaves on the dough, then the mozzarella, Fontina, tomato, mushrooms, blue cheese, herbs, and Parmesan.

3.   Bake until the dough is nicely browned, 10 to 12 minutes. Transfer onto a firm surface and cut with a pizza cutter or a large sharp knife. Serve immediately.

TO PREPARE AHEAD: Have all the ingredients ready and make the pizza just before you are ready to serve.

Spinach, Mushroom, and Blue Cheese Pizza makes a deliciously earthy and satisfying meal.

SAUTÉED VEGETABLE PIZZA

You can be creative with the vegetables you choose. However, the ones listed below make for a colorful as well as a delicious pizza. When sautéing the vegetables, do not overcook. Remember that they will be going back into the oven atop the pizza.

MAKES FOUR 8-INCH PIZZAS

About ½ cup extra-virgin olive oil

¼ pound fresh mushrooms, stemmed, cleaned, and thinly sliced (about 1½ cups)

Kosher salt and freshly ground black pepper

1 Asian eggplant (3 ounces), trimmed and thinly sliced

1 large or 2 small green zucchini (8 to 10 ounces), trimmed and cut into cubes

1 large or 2 small yellow zucchini (8 to 10 ounces), trimmed and cut into cubes

1 small red or yellow bell pepper (about 4 ounces), trimmed, seeded, and cut into thin slices

1 recipe Pizza Dough (see page 73)

2 tablespoons Chili and Garlic Oil (see page 20)

2 cups grated mozzarella cheese (8 ounces)

2 cups grated Fontina cheese (8 ounces)

1 pound Roma tomatoes, ends trimmed and sliced

4 teaspoons freshly grated Parmesan cheese

1.   In a small skillet, heat 2½ tablespoons of the olive oil. Sauté the mushrooms for 3 or 4 minutes, adding a bit more oil if necessary. The mushrooms should be al dente. Season lightly with salt and pepper, drain, and set aside.

2.   Wipe the skillet and heat 2 more tablespoons of the oil. Sauté the eggplant until al dente, 3 to 4 minutes. Season lightly with salt and pepper, drain, and set aside.

3. In a medium skillet, heat 2 more tablespoons of the oil. Sauté the green and yellow zucchini until al dente, about 3 minutes, adding a bit more oil as necessary. Season lightly with salt and pepper, drain, and set aside.

4. In a small skillet heat 1 tablespoon oil. Sauté the red or yellow pepper until al dente, about 2 minutes. Season lightly with salt and pepper, drain, and set aside.

5. Place a pizza stone on the middle rack of the oven and preheat the oven to 500°F.

6. To assemble the pizza, on a lightly floured surface stretch or roll out the dough into 8-inch rounds and brush the inner circle with Chili and Garlic Oil. Sprinkle each pizza first with ½ cup of the mozzarella, then with ½ cup of the Fontina. Divide the vegetables among the pizzas and layer with the sliced tomatoes, mushrooms, eggplant, zucchini, and peppers. Sprinkle 1 teaspoon Parmesan over the top of each pizza.

7. Slide each pizza gently onto the stone and bake until the crust is nicely browned, 10 to 12 minutes. Transfer the pizza onto a firm surface and cut into slices with a pizza cutter or a very sharp knife. Serve immediately.

TO PREPARE AHEAD: Through step 4, all the vegetables can be sautéed early in the day, cooled, and arranged in individual piles on a large platter. Refrigerate until needed.

SHRIMP AND GOAT CHEESE PIZZA

MAKES FOUR 8-INCH PIZZAS

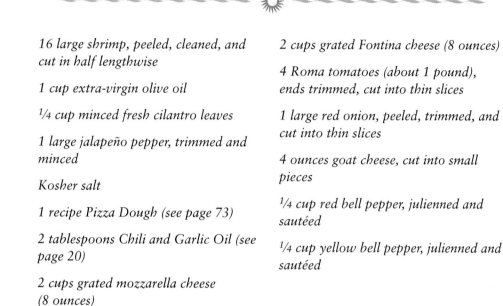

16 large shrimp, peeled, cleaned, and cut in half lengthwise

1 cup extra-virgin olive oil

¼ cup minced fresh cilantro leaves

1 large jalapeño pepper, trimmed and minced

Kosher salt

1 recipe Pizza Dough (see page 73)

2 tablespoons Chili and Garlic Oil (see page 20)

2 cups grated mozzarella cheese (8 ounces)

2 cups grated Fontina cheese (8 ounces)

4 Roma tomatoes (about 1 pound), ends trimmed, cut into thin slices

1 large red onion, peeled, trimmed, and cut into thin slices

4 ounces goat cheese, cut into small pieces

¼ cup red bell pepper, julienned and sautéed

¼ cup yellow bell pepper, julienned and sautéed

1. Prepare the shrimp: In a large shallow bowl, combine the shrimp with the olive oil, cilantro, jalapeño, and salt, turning to coat and flavor well. Marinate for 30 minutes in the refrigerator.

2. Heat a skillet or sauté pan large enough to hold the shrimp in one layer, and spoon 1 tablespoon of the oil from the marinade into the skillet. Carefully arrange the shrimp in the skillet and, over high heat, sauté just to color, 30 or 40 seconds per side. (Do not overcook, as it will continue to cook on top of pizza dough.) Remove with a slotted spoon and set aside to cool. Season lightly with salt before arranging on the pizza dough.

3. Place a pizza stone on the middle rack of the oven and preheat the oven to 500°F.

4.   On a lightly floured surface, stretch or roll out the dough to four 8-inch rounds, with the outer border a little thicker than the inner circle. Brush each of the pizza rounds with the Chili and Garlic Oil.

5.   Layer the pizza: Start with the mozzarella, then the Fontina, tomato, onion, shrimp, goat cheese, and red and yellow peppers.

6.   Gently slide the pizza onto the baking stone and bake until crust is golden brown, about 10 to 12 minutes.

7.   Transfer the pizza onto a firm surface and cut into slices with a pizza cutter or a very sharp knife. Serve immediately.

TO PREPARE AHEAD: All the ingredients can be readied early in the day and refrigerated, covered, until needed.

CHEESELESS PIZZA

I love to make this pizza in the summertime when the tomatoes are ripe off the vine and as sweet as can be. Eat it hot out of the oven, or try it the way I like it: Allow it to cool for a few minutes and drizzle some balsamic vinegar and extra-virgin olive oil over the top.

MAKES ONE 8-INCH PIZZA; SERVES 1 OR 2

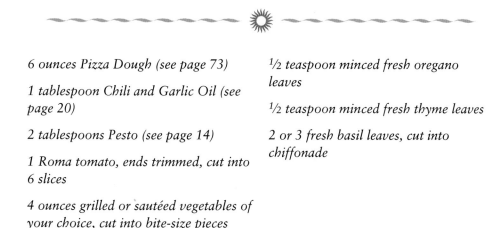

6 ounces Pizza Dough (see page 73)

1 tablespoon Chili and Garlic Oil (see page 20)

2 tablespoons Pesto (see page 14)

1 Roma tomato, ends trimmed, cut into 6 slices

4 ounces grilled or sautéed vegetables of your choice, cut into bite-size pieces

½ teaspoon minced fresh oregano leaves

½ teaspoon minced fresh thyme leaves

2 or 3 fresh basil leaves, cut into chiffonade

1. Place a pizza stone on the middle rack of the oven and preheat the oven to 500°F.

2. On a lightly floured surface, stretch or roll out the dough to a 8-inch round and brush the inner circle with the Chili and Garlic Oil. Bake the dough until it is very lightly brown, about 5 minutes.

3. Carefully remove the dough from the oven and while it is still on the peel or rimless baking tray, brush the dough with the Pesto, arrange the sliced tomatoes on the pizza, and top with the grilled vegetables, oregano, and thyme. Return the pizza to the oven and bake until crust is nicely browned, 6 to 7 more minutes.

4. Carefully remove the pizza from the oven and transfer onto a firm surface.

5. To serve, garnish with the basil, cut into slices, and serve immediately.

BRUNCH PIZZA WITH SCRAMBLED EGGS AND SMOKED SALMON

The Italians have a pasta called carbonara, which they make with bacon and eggs. If they can eat breakfast on their pasta, then why not on a pizza? The eggs get scrambled very lightly and then spread onto the pizza and covered with smoked salmon and caviar. Served any time of the day, this pizza hits the spot.

Be sure to cool the eggs after they are scrambled to prevent the pizza dough from becoming soft, making it impossible to transfer to the pizza stone.

MAKES ONE 8-INCH PIZZA; SERVES 1 TO 2

4 large eggs

¼ cup milk or half-and-half

Kosher salt and freshly ground white pepper

4 tablespoons (½ stick) unsalted butter, cut into small pieces

6 ounces Pizza Dough (see page 73)

1 tablespoon Chili and Garlic Oil (see page 20)

¼ cup grated mozzarella cheese (1 ounce)

¼ cup grated Fontina cheese (1 ounce)

2 ounces smoked salmon, cut into very thin slices

Chopped chives, for garnish

1 to 2 teaspoons caviar or salmon roe, optional

1.   Place a pizza stone on the middle rack of the oven and preheat the oven to 500°F.

2.   In a medium bowl, whisk together the eggs, milk, salt, and pepper. In a 10-inch skillet, melt the butter. Over very low heat, scramble the egg mixture until it is still very soft and slightly runny. (Keep in mind that the eggs will continue to cook when the pizza goes into the oven.) Remove from the heat and cool completely.

3.   On a lightly floured surface, stretch or roll out the dough to an 8-inch round and brush the Chili and Garlic Oil over the inner circle. Spread the cooled eggs on the dough, within ½ inch of the edges; scatter the mozzarella cheese, then the

Fontina cheese, evenly over the eggs; and transfer to the pizza stone. Bake until the crust is golden brown, about 10 to 12 minutes. (The eggs will have puffed up.)

4.   Carefully remove the pizza from the oven and transfer onto a firm surface, arrange the slices of smoked salmon on the eggs, covering the entire pizza, and garnish with the chopped chives.

5.   To serve, using a pizza cutter or a large sharp knife, cut the pizza into 4 or 6 slices and, if desired, spoon a little of the caviar in the center of each slice. Serve immediately.

TO PREPARE AHEAD: Through step 2. The eggs can be scrambled and allowed to cool. Continue with the recipe when ready to serve.

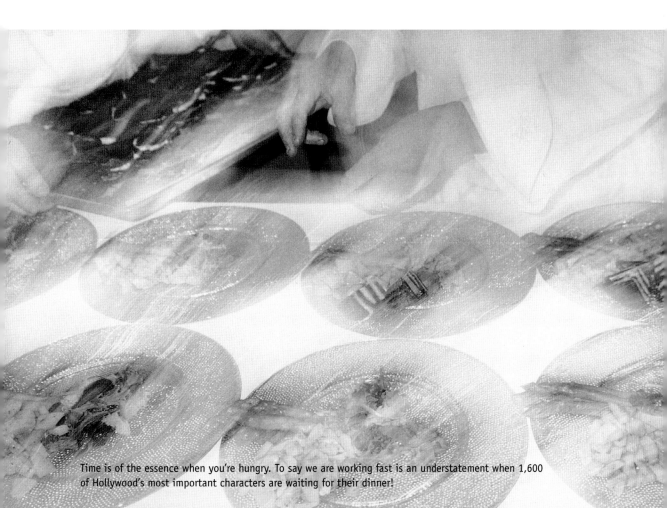

Time is of the essence when you're hungry. To say we are working fast is an understatement when 1,600 of Hollywood's most important characters are waiting for their dinner!

CALZONE WITH FOUR CHEESES
AND BLACK TRUFFLES

Unlike white truffles, black truffles must be warmed up or cooked to bring out their full flavor. As the high heat in the oven melts the cheese, it is instantly saturated with the intense black truffle flavor. When you cut into this calzone, the wonderful aroma will dazzle you.

MAKES 2 SMALL CALZONES; SERVES 1 TO 2

½ cup grated mozzarella cheese

½ cup goat cheese

⅓ cup mascarpone cheese

⅓ cup freshly grated Parmesan cheese

1 egg, lightly beaten

¼ teaspoon minced fresh thyme leaves

Pinch of freshly ground black pepper

*Slices of black truffles, to taste

12 ounces Pizza Dough (see page 73)

1 to 2 tablespoons extra-virgin olive oil

1.   Place a pizza stone on the middle rack of the oven and preheat the oven to 500°F.

2.   In a small bowl, combine the mozzarella, goat, mascarpone, and Parmesan cheeses, the egg, minced thyme, and pepper. Mix well. Carefully stir in slices of black truffles.

3.   On a lightly floured surface, stretch or roll out the dough into two 8-inch circles. Spread the filling on half of each circle, leaving about a 1-inch margin around the edge. Moisten the edge of the dough with water and fold the half without the filling over to enclose the truffles-and-cheese mixture, pinching the edges together to seal tightly.

4.   Transfer the calzones to the pizza stone and bake until they are nicely browned, about 10 to 12 minutes. Carefully remove them from the oven to a serving plate and brush with olive oil. Serve immediately.

---

*You can substitute the fresh slices of black truffles with ⅓ cup sautéed wild mushrooms seasoned with truffle oil.

The incredible black-truffle aroma explodes when this calzone is sliced in half.

VEGETABLE CALZONE

This recipe makes one small calzone. If you want a larger one, roll out 12 ounces of the dough into a 12- or 14-inch circle and use twice as much of the filling. The dough will puff up as it bakes, making for a very impressive presentation.

MAKES 1 SMALL CALZONE; SERVES 1

---

6 ounces Pizza Dough (see page 73)

1/2 cup grated mozzarella cheese (2 ounces)

1/2 cup grated Fontina cheese (2 ounces)

1 cup spinach leaves, washed, dried, and stemmed

1/2 cup sliced shiitake mushrooms, sautéed

1/4 cup sliced Asian eggplant rounds, sautéed

2 tablespoons freshly grated Parmesan cheese

1 to 2 tablespoons extra-virgin olive oil

1. Place a pizza stone on the middle rack of the oven and preheat the oven to 500°F.

2. On a lightly floured surface, stretch or roll out the dough to an 8-inch circle. Layer the filling on half the circle, leaving about a 1-inch margin around the edge. Start with the mozzarella, then the Fontina, spinach, mushrooms, eggplant, and Parmesan. Moisten the edge of the dough with water and fold the top half over to enclose the filling, pinching the edges together to seal tightly.

3. Transfer the calzone to the pizza stone and bake until the calzone is nicely browned, about 12 minutes. Carefully remove it from the oven to a serving platter and brush with olive oil. Serve immediately.

I think we got the last of the season's black truffles shipped to us—forty pounds from France for the Governor's Ball after the Oscars.

WP
PASTA

When Barbara and I opened our first restaurant, Spago, in 1982, our customers couldn't get enough pasta. Today, despite all the silly diets and the anticarbohydrate craze, pasta is still as popular as ever. Even in Los Angeles, a city of fickle appetites, it always sells. It has become the favorite comfort food of Americans. As long as you choose fresh, quality ingredients, it's hard to go wrong with pasta.

Sometimes I prefer a very simple pasta dish with only two ingredients in it, but other times I'm in the mood for something more complex in flavor. Penne with Fresh Peas and Prosciutto (see page 157) is the dish to make when you're busy and don't have a lot of time to shop and prepare. But if you're entertaining and want to impress your friends, try my Angel Hair with Crabmeat, Oven-Dried Tomatoes, Asparagus, and Golden Caviar (see page 125). For a traditional Italian dish, make the Angel Hair with Wild Mushrooms, Asparagus, and Shaved Parmesan Cheese (see page 133). But for something more exotic, try Fettuccine with Lobster and Green Curry Sauce (see page 146). Complex but clean, the tastes change and evolve in your mouth. Serve it as an appetizer or as a main course.

I urge you to make fresh pasta at home whenever possible. Over the years my staff and I have tried many different pasta dough recipes. Though it took us fifteen years, we finally got it right. The one in this chapter—and its variations—is our favorite so far. Most homemade pasta ends up starchy and overcooked and clumps together. This pasta won't overcook as easily as other recipes, and is a beautiful, bright yellow hue. Made with a higher proportion of egg yolks and just the smallest amount of water, it retains its firm, dense texture even after it has been cooked. Of course, it's not my invention! The Italians have known about the egg yolk secret for hundreds of years. At first it may seem like too many egg yolks, but you'll see that it's not. The most important thing is the cooking time. This dough takes a bit longer than others to cook, but if you take the time to make it, I'm sure you'll agree that the difference in flavor and texture is immeasurable.

Pasta can be made in a mixer, in a food processor, or by hand. The pasta can be rolled out and cut by hand or rolled through and cut with a pasta machine. Both methods are equally successful if directions are followed.

To make perfectly cooked pasta, there are just a few basic rules to follow. For every pound of pasta, use 4 quarts of cold water. Bring the water to a boil over high heat, add salt, and when the water comes back to a rolling boil, add the pasta. Lower the heat slightly, stir the pasta gently with a long-handled spoon or fork, and cook until the pasta is al dente, or "firm to the tooth." It will take a shorter time to cook homemade pasta than store-bought. The thinner noodle can cook anywhere from 1 to 3 minutes, depending upon the dryness of the pasta. For store-bought pasta, follow the directions on the package.

To make pasta by hand, heap the flour in a mound on the worktable, making a well in the center. Break the eggs into the well, add the salt and olive oil, and gently whisk with a fork. Gradually bring the flour into the eggs until almost all the flour is incorporated. Then knead for about 10 minutes, using your fingers and the heel of your hand, until the dough is smooth and elastic. Divide the dough into 3 or 4 pieces, wrap each piece in plastic wrap, and let the dough rest for 30 minutes.

To roll out the dough by hand, sprinkle the worktable lightly with flour. Using a good rolling pin, roll out the first piece of dough, first in one direction, then turn the dough and roll in the other direction until the dough is stretched to the desired thickness. To turn the dough, roll it around the rolling pin and then unroll so that the side of the dough formerly at the bottom is now on the top. Try to keep the thickness of the dough as even as possible.

To cut into noodles, bring the long ends together to meet at the center. Sprinkle lightly with flour and repeat folding toward the center two more times (see photo on page 112). Using a sharp knife, cut the dough into the size noodles desired. Slip the dull edge of the knife under the center of the dough and let the noodles separate (see photo on page 112).

To make the noodles with a hand-cranked pasta machine, flatten a ball of dough as much as possible. Set the machine at its widest opening and then start to run the dough through. (The dough will come out in many pieces this first time.) Lay them flat and press the pieces together. Run through three, four, or as many times as necessary, until the dough is nice and smooth, each time folding the dough into thirds, the width a little smaller than the width of the roller. Then start to stretch the dough, narrowing the setting each time you pass the dough through. If, after the second or third setting, the length of the dough becomes too unmanageable, cut the dough in half and run each half through separately. (This applies as well to dough when you are making ravioli.) If you find the dough is getting too thin, stop before the last setting. If you want a thinner noodle, run the dough through the last setting twice.

Before cutting into noodles, lightly flour the dough to prevent the noodles from sticking together. You may want to cut the lengths of dough in half, which will make it easier to cut into noodles and will make the noodles easier to mix with sauces.

To make ravioli, cut the dough into strips 5 inches wide and 16 to 18 inches long. Brush the bottom half of the dough lightly with egg wash and spoon about 1 teaspoon of filling at 1½- to 2-inch intervals along the egg-washed side. Fold the top half of the dough over so that the ends meet and press the edges firmly together. Trim the edges as necessary. Crimp around the filling with the outside of your hands and then cut into ravioli with a serrated or plain-edged pasta cutter or a large, sharp knife.

To make round ravioli, use a 3- or 4-inch cookie cutter and cut out the ravioli. To make half-moon shapes, cut out the rounds, place the filling in the center, brush the edges with egg wash, and fold in half.

To make tortellini, using the half-moon shape, wrap the filled and folded pasta around your finger and press one end over the other.

To make cappelletti ("little hats"), cut the dough into 2-inch squares. Place a scant teaspoon of filling in the center of the square, brush the edges with egg wash, and fold two opposite corners together and seal, forming a triangle. Wrap the triangle around your finger, pressing one end on top of the other.

As the pasta is cut into whatever form or shape you choose, sprinkle a baking tray with semolina flour and arrange the finished pasta on the tray, sprinkling additional flour over so that the pasta can dry. When dry, the pasta can be used as needed or put into plastic containers and frozen for up to one month for future use. Cook directly from the freezer.

TYPES OF NOODLES

Angel hair: A long, thin strand of pasta, probably called angel hair because of the fineness of the noodle.

Cannelloni: A large tubular pasta that can be stuffed with a variety of fillings—meat, cheese, vegetable purée, or a combination.

Farfalle: Shaped like a bow tie, farfalle can have straight or ridged edges.

Fettuccine: This is a long, flat noodle, the Roman version of tagliatelle.

Lasagna noodles: Flat, wide sheets of dough with straight or ridged edges. If the pasta is homemade, make the noodle slightly smaller than the size of the pan being used.

Linguine: A long, thin, flat noodle that is wider than angel hair and thinner than fettuccine.

Pappardelle: An inch-wide flat noodle that lends itself to sauces that are a bit heavier, such as a Bolognese sauce, with chicken or meat.

Penne: A tubular pasta that comes plain or ribbed. The ends are cut at an angle, like a quill.

Rigatoni: A short, tubular macaroni, usually ribbed.

Spaghetti: The most familiar form of pasta, spaghetti is a long strand that can be thin or thick.

Stuffed pasta: Examples are ravioli, cappelletti, tortellini. Ravioli can be square or round or half-moon shaped; cappelletti are shaped like little peaked hats; and tortellini are stuffed rounds of dough that are folded in half, the ends brought together, forming a circle of dough with a hole in the center. The stuffing can be meat, fish, chicken, cheese, vegetables, or a combination of any of the above.

Tagliatelle: A long, flat noodle, this is the Bolognese version of fettuccine. It combines well with meat or cream sauces.

Vermicelli: This is a thin spaghetti, a bit thicker than angel hair.

1.
Pour the eggs into the well in the mound of flour.

2.
Mixing with your hands, gradually begin to draw the flour into the eggs.

3.
Before cutting the noodles, bring the long ends of the sheets of dough together to meet at the center. Sprinkle lightly with flour and repeat the folding toward the center two more times.

4.
Using a fluted wheel or a knife, cut the pasta dough into the desired width for noodles. Slip the dull edge of a knife under the center of the dough and let the noodles separate.

BASIC PASTA DOUGH

Making pasta can be fun, and it is easy to involve the whole family in the preparation. The dough can be made with half semolina and half all-purpose flour, which will give you a firmer dough.

MAKES ABOUT 1½ POUNDS; SERVES 6 TO 8

3 cups all-purpose flour

8 large egg yolks

1 teaspoon kosher salt

1 teaspoon extra-virgin olive oil

2 to 3 tablespoons water

Semolina or all-purpose flour, for dusting

1. In a food processor fitted with the steel blade, combine the flour, egg yolks, salt, olive oil, and 2 tablespoons of the water. Process until the dough begins to hold together, then stop the machine and pinch the dough to test it. If it is too dry, add up to 1 more tablespoon of water and process until it forms a moist ball. Turn out onto a lightly floured smooth work surface and knead by hand, until a smooth ball is formed. Loosely wrap in plastic wrap and let rest at room temperature for 30 minutes to 1 hour.

2. Cut the dough into 4 equal pieces. Keep the other pieces covered in plastic while you roll out one piece at a time, by hand with a rolling pin or through the rollers of a pasta machine, stretching the dough to the desired thickness.

3. If using a pasta machine, set the rollers at the widest opening. Flatten the first piece of dough into a thick strip no wider than the machine, to enable it to pass through the rollers. If necessary, dust the pasta very lightly with flour. Run the pasta through the machine. Fold in thirds, crosswise, and run through the machine again. Repeat this procedure two or more times, until the dough is smooth and somewhat elastic. Set the machine to the next smaller opening and run the dough through the rollers. Continue rolling and stretching the dough, using the smaller opening each time, until the next to the last or the last opening is reached, dusting lightly

with flour only as necessary. (The strip of dough will be long. If you don't have enough space on your worktable, halfway through the rolling process cut the strip of dough in half and continue to work with each piece separately, keeping the unused dough covered.)

4.   Adjust the cutting mechanism to the desired width, cut the noodles, and allow them to dry before cooking. A convenient way to dry pasta is to arrange the cut pasta on a pastry tray sprinkled with flour, preferably semolina flour. As one layer is completed, sprinkle flour over the noodles, place a piece of parchment paper over them, and continue layering with noodles and flour. Dry for at least 15 to 20 minutes.

5.   Repeat with the remaining pieces of dough.

TO PREPARE AHEAD: Through step 1 and step 5. Fresh pasta will keep, refrigerated, for up to 3 days.

HERB PASTA DOUGH

MAKES ABOUT 1½ POUNDS; SERVES 6 TO 8

1 tablespoon finely chopped fresh thyme leaves

1 tablespoon finely chopped fresh rosemary leaves

1 tablespoon finely chopped fresh sage leaves

3 cups all-purpose flour

5 large egg yolks

1 teaspoon kosher salt

1 teaspoon extra-virgin olive oil

1 tablespoon water, if needed

Semolina or all-purpose flour, for dusting

1. Prepare the herb tea: In a very small saucepan, bring ½ cup water to a boil. Add the herbs and bring back to a boil. Lower the heat and reduce to ¼ cup. Remove the pan from the heat, cover, and let steep for 15 minutes. Cool.

2. In a food processor fitted with the steel blade, place the flour, the egg yolks, the salt, the olive oil, and the herb tea. Process until the dough begins to hold together, then stop the machine and pinch the dough to test it. If it is too dry, add 1 table-spoon of water and process until it forms a moist ball. Turn out onto a lightly floured work surface and knead by hand, forming a smooth ball. Loosely wrap the dough in plastic wrap and let rest at room temperature for 30 minutes.

3. Cut the dough into 4 equal pieces. Keep the other pieces covered in plastic while you roll out one piece at a time, by hand with a rolling pin or through the rollers of a pasta machine, stretching the dough to the desired thickness.

4. If using a pasta machine, set the rollers at the widest opening. Flatten the first piece of dough into a thick strip no wider than the machine, to enable it to pass through the rollers. If necessary, dust the pasta very lightly with flour. Run the pasta through the machine. Fold in thirds, crosswise, and run through the machine again. Repeat this procedure two or more times, until the dough is smooth and somewhat elastic. Set the machine to the next smaller opening and run the dough through the

rollers. Continue rolling and stretching the dough, using the smaller opening each time, until the next to the last or the last opening is reached, dusting lightly with flour only as necessary. (The strip of dough will be long. If you don't have enough space on your worktable, halfway through the rolling process cut the strip of dough in half and continue to work with each piece separately, keeping the unused dough covered.)

5. Adjust the cutting mechanism to the desired width, cut the noodles, and allow them to dry before cooking. A convenient way to dry pasta is to arrange the cut pasta on a pastry tray sprinkled with flour, preferably semolina flour. As one layer is completed, sprinkle flour over the noodles, place a piece of parchment paper over them, and continue layering with noodles and flour. Dry for at least 15 to 20 minutes.

6. Repeat with the remaining pieces of dough.

TO PREPARE AHEAD: Through step 6. Fresh pasta will keep, refrigerated, for up to 3 days.

SPINACH PASTA DOUGH

MAKES ABOUT 1½ POUNDS; SERVES 6 TO 8

* * *

½ pound fresh spinach (about 1 bunch), washed, dried, and stemmed

3 cups semolina or all-purpose flour

5 egg yolks

1 teaspoon kosher salt

1 teaspoon extra-virgin olive oil

1 tablespoon water, if needed

1. Coarsely chop and then purée the spinach in a food processor fitted with the steel blade. Transfer the purée to a linen towel or napkin, close the towel, and squeeze out the juice into a measuring cup. There should be about ¼ cup juice. (Wash the towel or napkin and save for just this purpose, since the spinach may leave a permanent stain.) Stir 2 tablespoons of the purée into the juice and reserve. The remaining purée can be used as desired.

2. In a food processor fitted with the steel blade, combine the flour, the egg yolks, salt, olive oil, and reserved spinach juice mixture and process until the dough begins to hold together. Stop the machine and pinch the dough to test it. If it is too dry, add a little water and process until it forms a moist ball. Turn out onto a lightly floured surface and knead by hand until a smooth ball is formed. Loosely wrap the dough in plastic wrap and let rest at room temperature for 30 minutes.

3. Cut the dough into 4 equal pieces. Keep the other pieces covered in plastic while you roll out one piece at a time, by hand with a rolling pin or through the rollers of a pasta machine, stretching the dough to the desired thickness.

4. If using a pasta machine, set the rollers at the widest opening. Flatten the first piece of dough into a thick strip no wider than the machine, to enable it to pass through the rollers. If necessary, dust the pasta very lightly with flour. Run the pasta through the machine. Fold in thirds, crosswise, and run through the machine again. Repeat this procedure two or more times, until the dough is smooth and somewhat elastic. Set the machine to the next smaller opening and run the dough through the

rollers. Continue rolling and stretching the dough, using the smaller opening each time, until the next to the last or the last opening is reached, dusting lightly with flour only as necessary. (The strip of dough will be long. If you don't have enough space on your worktable, halfway through the rolling process cut the strip of dough in half and continue to work with each piece separately, keeping the unused dough covered.)

5.   Adjust the cutting mechanism to the desired width, cut the noodles, and allow them to dry before cooking. A convenient way to dry pasta is to arrange the cut pasta on a pastry tray sprinkled with flour, preferably semolina flour. As one layer is completed, sprinkle flour over the noodles, place a piece of parchment paper over them, and continue layering with noodles and flour. Dry for at least 15 to 20 minutes.

6.   Repeat with the remaining pieces of dough.

TO PREPARE AHEAD: Through step 6. Fresh pasta will keep, refrigerated, for up to 3 days.

SPICY RED PEPPER PASTA DOUGH

MAKES ABOUT 1½ POUNDS; SERVES 6 TO 8

1 medium red bell pepper (6 ounces)

3 cups semolina or all-purpose flour

5 egg yolks

1 teaspoon kosher salt

1 teaspoon extra-virgin olive oil

1 teaspoon red pepper flakes, chopped fine

1 tablespoon of water, if needed

Semolina flour, for dusting

1.   Roast the red pepper on a grill, under the broiler, or on top of the stove until the skin is blackened all over. Place the pepper in a paper bag, close the bag, and let the pepper steam for about 10 minutes. Remove the pepper and peel away the charred skin. Core and seed the pepper, and cut it into pieces. Purée the pepper in a food processor fitted with the steel blade. (You should have about ¼ cup purée.) Set aside.

2.   In the same bowl of the food processor (it's not necessary to clean the bowl), combine the flour, egg yolks, salt, olive oil, pepper flakes, and the puréed red pepper and process until the dough begins to hold together. Stop the machine and pinch the dough to test it. If it is too dry, add a little water and process until it forms a moist ball. Turn out onto a lightly floured work surface and knead by hand until a smooth ball is formed. Loosely wrap the dough in plastic wrap and let it rest at room temperature for 30 minutes.

3.   Cut the dough into 4 equal pieces. Keep the other pieces covered in plastic while you roll out one piece at a time, by hand with a rolling pin or through the rollers of a pasta machine, stretching the dough to the desired thickness.

4.   If using a pasta machine, set the rollers at the widest opening. Flatten the first piece of dough into a thick strip no wider than the machine, to enable it to pass through the rollers. If necessary, dust the pasta very lightly with flour. Run the pasta

through the machine. Fold in thirds, crosswise, and run through the machine again. Repeat this procedure two or more times, until the dough is smooth and somewhat elastic. Set the machine to the next smaller opening and run the dough through the rollers. Continue rolling and stretching the dough, using the smaller opening each time, until the next to the last or the last opening is reached, dusting lightly with flour only as necessary. (The strip of dough will be long. If you don't have enough space on your worktable, halfway through the rolling process cut the strip of dough in half and continue to work with each piece separately, keeping the unused dough covered.)

5.   Adjust the cutting mechanism to the desired width, cut the noodles, and allow them to dry before cooking. A convenient way to dry pasta is to arrange the cut pasta on a pastry tray sprinkled with flour, preferably semolina flour. As one layer is completed, sprinkle flour over the noodles, place a piece of parchment paper over them, and continue layering with noodles and flour. Dry for at least 15 to 20 minutes.

6.   Repeat with the remaining pieces of dough.

POTATO GNOCCHI

MAKES 18 TO 20 OUNCES OF DOUGH

(FOR ABOUT 120 1-INCH GNOCCHI)

2 large baking potatoes, peeled and quartered

½ to ⅔ cup all-purpose flour

2 tablespoons freshly grated Parmesan cheese

1 egg, lightly beaten (use half only, discard remaining half)

Kosher salt

Freshly ground white pepper

Semolina or all-purpose flour, for dusting

1.   Cook the potatoes in boiling, salted water until fork tender, about 25 to 30 minutes. Drain. Over a medium bowl, pass through a ricer. Cool to room temperature.

2.   Transfer the potato to the lightly floured surface of a worktable. Sprinkle ½ cup of the flour and the cheese over the potato. Make a well in the center and place half of the beaten egg, salt, and pepper. Start stirring the potato mixture into the egg mixture and continue to mix until it begins to form a ball, being careful not to over-work the dough. If the dough is wet and hard to handle, add the remaining flour. To test for texture, shape one or two gnocchi and put into a small pan of boiling salted water. If they fall apart, a little more flour is needed, but add only a small amount at a time.

3.   To shape the gnocchi: Divide the dough into 8 portions. On a lightly floured surface, roll each piece of dough into a long rope, about ¼ inch by 15 inches. Cut into one-inch pieces (or into traditional gnocchi shape). Line a baking tray with parchment paper, and lightly dust with flour. Arrange the gnocchi in one layer and set aside until ready to use, up to two hours at room temperature.

4.   To cook gnocchi: Bring a large stockpot of salted water to a boil. Divide the gnocchi into 4 batches and add one batch, cooking until gnocchi rise to the surface,

about 1 to 2 minutes. Remove with a slotted spoon and repeat with the remaining 3 batches. Use as needed.

Every plate must be perfect.

ANGEL HAIR WITH FRESH TOMATO, BASIL, AND GARLIC

When tomatoes are out of season and not as sweet as they should be, a pinch of sugar or a little honey will enhance the flavor. Olives, capers, dried tomatoes, and/or chili peppers can also be added if desired.

SERVES 4

✳

TOMATO BASE*

2 tablespoons extra-virgin olive oil

1 tablespoon chopped garlic

2 teaspoons chopped shallots

4 cups tomato concasse** (made with 2 pounds whole tomatoes)

1 tablespoon sugar or honey, optional

1 teaspoon kosher salt

2 teaspoons tomato paste

1 teaspoon chopped fresh thyme leaves

SAUCE

¼ cup extra-virgin olive oil

5 ounces Double-Blanched Garlic, sliced (see page 30)

2 cups tomato concasse (made with 1 pound whole tomatoes)

2 cups Tomato Base

¼ cup chopped fresh basil leaves

¼ teaspoon kosher salt

12 ounces fresh or store-bought angel-hair pasta

¼ cup chopped fresh flat-leaf parsley leaves

Chopped fresh basil leaves

Freshly grated Parmesan cheese

---

*Tomato Base can be made in large quantities and frozen for up to 3 months, to be used to improve sauces made with tomatoes. This recipe makes about 2 cups.

**Tomato concasse is nothing more than peeled, seeded, and chopped tomatoes. To peel, remove the core of the tomato, score the bottom with an X, and carefully slide into a pan of simmering water to cover. When the skin just begins to peel away (which could take as little as 10 seconds, depending upon the ripeness of the tomato), remove the tomato with a slotted spoon and immediately refresh it under cold water. Peel away the outer skin, cut the tomato in half across the middle, and squeeze each half to remove the seeds. Then, coarsely chop the tomato with a heavy knife.

1.   Make the Tomato Base: In a 12-inch skillet, heat the olive oil. Sauté the garlic and shallots just until they start to color. Add the 4 cups of tomato concasse, sugar, if necessary, and salt and cook over medium heat until reduced by half, stirring occasionally. Stir in the tomato paste and chopped thyme and set aside.

2.   Bring a large stockpot of water to a boil.

3.   Make the sauce: In a clean 12-inch skillet or sauté pan, heat the olive oil. Over medium-high heat, sauté the garlic, stirring often, until it is lightly golden in color, about 2 minutes.

4.   Remove the skillet from the heat and stir in the 2 cups of tomato concasse, the reserved 2 cups of Tomato Base, the ¼ cup chopped basil, and the salt. Return the skillet to the heat and simmer over medium-high heat until some of the moisture from the tomatoes evaporates, 3 to 4 minutes.

5.   When ready to serve, add salt to the pot of boiling water and cook the pasta until it is al dente, about 1 minute for fresh pasta (cook packaged pasta according to the directions on the box). Drain the pasta and add it to the sauce with the chopped fresh parsley. Gently stir to heat through and to coat the pasta with sauce.

6.   To serve, divide the pasta and sauce evenly among 4 large, warm plates or bowls. Garnish with chopped basil and grated Parmesan cheese.

TO PREPARE AHEAD: Through step 4. When ready to serve, warm the sauce over low heat.

ANGEL HAIR WITH CRABMEAT, OVEN-DRIED TOMATOES, ASPARAGUS, AND GOLDEN CAVIAR

This very elegant pasta dish always takes people by surprise. The color and flavor of the crab, the texture of the caviar, and the bright green asparagus make a beautiful presentation. Look for my favorite crabs—Dungeness—when they are in season.

SERVES 4

8 tablespoons (1 stick) unsalted butter, cut into small pieces

2 tablespoons chopped shallots

1 tablespoon chopped garlic

½ cup Oven-Dried Tomatoes (see page 26), cut into bite-size pieces

2 cups homemade Chicken Stock (see page 4) or store-bought, heated

½ cup heavy cream

Kosher salt and freshly ground black pepper

12 ounces fresh or store-bought angel-hair pasta

8 ounces jumbo lump crabmeat

⅓ cup freshly grated Parmesan cheese

1 tablespoon chopped fresh basil leaves, plus 8 whole leaves for garnish

¼ cup chopped fresh flat-leaf parsley leaves

20 medium asparagus tips (2 to 3 inches long), blanched, refreshed in cold water, and gently dried on toweling

1 tablespoon plus 1 teaspoon golden caviar, optional

Whole basil leaves, for garnish

1. Bring a large stockpot of water to a boil. Season with salt.

2. In a large skillet or sauté pan, melt the butter. Over medium heat, sauté the shallots and garlic until golden. Stir in the tomatoes and pour in the stock and cream. Season lightly with salt and pepper. Reduce by half.

3. While the sauce is reducing, add salt to the pot of boiling water and cook the pasta until it is al dente, about 1 minute for fresh pasta. (Cook packaged pasta ac-

cording to the directions on the box.) Drain the pasta well and add it to the sauce with the crabmeat, tossing the mixture well to heat through and coat with the sauce.

4.   Remove from the heat, stir in the cheese, basil, and parsley, and adjust the seasoning to taste.

5.   To serve, divide and mound the pasta in the center of 4 large heated plates. Place 5 asparagus spears onto each mound, top each portion with 1 teaspoon of golden caviar, if desired, and garnish with a few whole basil leaves. Serve immediately.

TO PREPARE AHEAD: Through step 2, about 1 hour before dinner. When ready to serve, warm the sauce over low heat and continue with the recipe.

This Angel Hair with Crabmeat, Oven-Dried Tomatoes, Asparagus, and Golden Caviar is called for on a special occasion.

ANGEL HAIR WITH GOAT CHEESE, BROCCOLI, AND TOASTED PINE NUTS

This was the first pasta dish we put on the menu at Spago in 1982. In those days we didn't even have a pasta machine—Mark Peel cut all of the noodles by hand. Some days they looked like delicate angel hair and some days they turned out like fettuccine. But in the end, people didn't care about the shape as much as the taste. Though it's no longer printed on our menu, we still have customers who ask for this classic Spago dish.

SERVES 4 TO 6

1 tablespoon extra-virgin olive oil

3 cups broccoli florets (³/4 pound)

Kosher salt and freshly ground black pepper

1½ cups homemade Chicken Stock (see page 4) or store-bought, heated

1 teaspoon fresh thyme leaves (or fresh basil), plus 4 to 6 sprigs, for garnish

4 tablespoons (½ stick) unsalted butter, cut into small pieces

4 ounces goat cheese, crumbled

12 ounces fresh or store-bought angel-hair pasta

2 tablespoons toasted pine nuts*

1. Bring a large stockpot of water to a boil.

2. In a 12-inch sauté pan, heat the tablespoon of olive oil. Over medium-high heat, sauté the broccoli florets, stirring as necessary, 2 to 3 minutes. Season lightly with salt and pepper. Transfer to a bowl and reserve until needed.

3. Deglaze the pan with the stock, and add the thyme leaves. Bring to a boil and reduce by half. Add the butter and the goat cheese and stir together until the cheese melts. Keep warm.

---

*To toast pine nuts, place the nuts in a small skillet in a single layer. Over low heat, toast until lightly golden, stirring often to prevent burning. This takes 3 or 4 minutes. Drain on paper towels.

4.   Meanwhile, add a little salt to the pot of boiling water and cook the pasta until it is al dente, about 1 minute for fresh pasta. (Cook packaged pasta according to the directions on the box.) Drain the pasta well and add to the reserved broccoli in the sauté pan. Cook until heated through, about 2 minutes. Season with salt and pepper to taste.

5.   To serve, divide the pasta among 4 heated plates. Sprinkle with toasted pine nuts and garnish with a sprig of thyme.

TO PREPARE AHEAD: Noodles can be cut 1 day ahead and refrigerated, covered with parchment or wax paper.

ANGEL HAIR WITH CHANTERELLES, FAVA BEANS, AND FRESH THYME

The earthy, robust flavors of the mushrooms alongside the beans and herbs make this springtime pasta dish comforting and satisfying. In the fall, I use lima or cranberry beans. They're so delicious, especially when you blanch them and peel off the skins. And if you can't find chanterelles, look for fresh morels or porcinis. If you feel extravagant, sprinkle a few drops of truffle oil on the pasta and grate a bit more cheese over each portion just before serving.

SERVES 4

1/2 pound chanterelle mushrooms (or any fresh assorted wild mushrooms), stemmed and wiped clean

1/4 cup extra-virgin olive oil

2 tablespoons minced garlic

2 tablespoons minched shallots

1 1/2 cups homemade Chicken Stock (see page 4) or Vegetable Stock (see page 6) or store-bought, heated

4 ounces (1 stick) unsalted butter, cut into small pieces

Kosher salt and freshly ground black pepper

8 ounces shelled fava beans, peeled and blanched

1 tablespoon minced fresh thyme leaves, plus 4 sprigs of fresh thyme for garnish

12 ounces fresh or store-bought angel-hair pasta

2 heaping tablespoons coarsely chopped, fresh flat-leaf parsley leaves

1/2 cup freshly grated Parmesan cheese

1.   Bring a large stockpot of water to a boil.

2.   Cut the mushrooms into large, bite-size pieces. In a large skillet or sauté pan, heat the olive oil. Add the garlic, shallots, and mushrooms and cook over high heat to release the flavor, about 1 to 2 minutes. Deglaze with the Chicken Stock. Add the butter and continue to cook over high heat for 2 minutes longer. Season with salt and pepper.

3.   Add the beans and chopped thyme and reduce the liquid by half.

4.   Cook the pasta until it is al dente, about 1 minute for fresh pasta (cook packaged pasta according to the directions on the box), and drain it well. Add the pasta to the sauce and toss well so that the pasta absorbs the sauce. Stir in the parsley and remove from the heat. Sprinkle in the Parmesan cheese and toss again to combine thoroughly.

5.   To serve, divide the pasta among 4 large heated plates or bowls, spooning mushrooms and sauce equally over the pasta. Garnish with a sprig of thyme and serve immediately.

TO PREPARE AHEAD: Through step 1. The beans can be cooked the day before, the herbs chopped early in the day.

Angel Hair with Wild Mushrooms, Asparagus, and Shaved Parmesan Cheese is spring cooking at its best.

ANGEL HAIR WITH WILD MUSHROOMS, ASPARAGUS, AND SHAVED PARMESAN CHEESE

The Mushroom Base will keep refrigerated for three or four days. Frozen, it will keep up to one month. The base will improve the flavor of any dish made with mushrooms.

SERVES 4

―――――――――― ☀ ――――――――――

MUSHROOM BASE

2 tablespoons extra-virgin olive oil

6 garlic cloves, peeled and crushed

1/4 cup diced mirepoix (equal portions of carrots, celery, and onion)

2 teaspoons minced shallots

7 ounces mixed wild mushrooms (such as morels, shiitake, porcini), trimmed and roughly chopped

1 cup dry white wine

1 cup homemade Chicken Stock (see page 4) or store-bought

1/4 cup heavy cream

Pinch of chopped fresh thyme leaves

Kosher salt and freshly ground white pepper

SAUCE

2 tablespoons extra-virgin olive oil

3/4 pound wild mushrooms, trimmed and cut into bite-size pieces

1 tablespoon plus 1 teaspoon minced shallots

2 teaspoons minced garlic

4 tablespoons (1/2 stick) unsalted butter

1 1/2 cups homemade Chicken Stock (see page 4) or store-bought

1/2 teaspoon kosher salt

1/4 teaspoon freshly ground white pepper

16 medium asparagus spears, peeled and trimmed to 4-inch lengths

12 ounces fresh or store-bought angel-hair pasta

1/2 cup freshly grated Parmesan cheese

1/4 cup chopped fresh flat-leaf parsley leaves

2 teaspoons truffle oil,* optional

1 ounce thinly shaved Parmesan cheese

―――――――――――――――

*Truffle oil keeps well, refrigerated and covered. However, a little of the fragrance disappears each time the bottle is uncapped.

1. Make the Mushroom Base: In a large sauté pan, heat the olive oil. Over medium-high heat, sauté the garlic until lightly brown. Add the mirepoix, shallots, and mushrooms, and cook for about 2 minutes longer. Lower the heat, pour in the wine, and reduce until all the liquid is absorbed. Pour in the stock and reduce until about ¼ cup remains. Add the cream, thyme, salt, and pepper. Cool the mixture and purée it in a food processor or blender. (If the sauce is too thick, thin it with 1 table-spoon each of stock and cream.) Set aside until needed.

2. Bring a large pot of water to a boil. Season with salt.

3. Make the sauce: In a large skillet or sauté pan, heat the olive oil over high heat. Sauté the mushrooms to develop the flavor, about 2 minutes. Lower the heat, add the shallots, garlic, and butter, and continue to sauté, stirring occasionally, until the butter melts.

4. Pour in the stock and 2 tablespoons plus 2 teaspoons of the Mushroom Base. Bring the mixture to a boil, then lower to a simmer and cook for 2 to 3 minutes. Season with salt and pepper.

5. Blanch the asparagus in simmering salted water. Drain and keep warm.

6. Add the pasta to the large stockpot of boiling salted water and cook until it is al dente, about 1 minute for fresh pasta. (Cook packaged pasta according to the di-rections on the box.) Drain the pasta, add it to the sauce, and gently toss to coat well. Remove the mixture from the heat and stir in the grated Parmesan, chopped parsley, and, if desired, the truffle oil. Adjust the seasoning to taste.

7. To serve, divide the pasta, mushrooms, and sauce among 4 large warm plates. Spoon a little of the sauce over and arrange 4 asparagus spears on top of each serv-ing. Garnish with the shaved Parmesan and serve immediately.

TO PREPARE AHEAD: Through step 1.

BOW TIES WITH SPRING VEGETABLES, ROASTED GARLIC, AND GRATED PARMESAN CHEESE

SERVES 4

———————————————— ☀ ————————————————

2 tablespoons flavored oil from Roasted Garlic (see page 32)

½ recipe of Roasted Garlic (see page 32)

4 tablespoons (½ stick) unsalted butter, cut into small pieces

2 tablespoons Oven-Dried Tomatoes (see page 26)

2 cups homemade Chicken Stock (see page 4) or store-bought, heated

2 teaspoons chopped fresh oregano leaves

2 teaspoons chopped fresh thyme leaves

4 tablespoons chopped fresh flat-leaf parsley leaves

½ teaspoon kosher salt

Freshly ground white pepper

2 ounces haricots verts, trimmed

1 carrot trimmed and cut into thin slices

12 pencil asparagus cut into 2-inch slices

1 cup broccoli florets

½ cup fresh peas

12 ounces bow-tie pasta

½ cup freshly grated Parmesan cheese

1.   Bring a large stockpot of water to a boil.

2.   In a large skillet or sauté pan, heat the flavored oil. Add the roasted garlic, butter, tomatoes, and stock. Season with the oregano, thyme, 2 tablespoons of the parsley, salt, and pepper, and reduce until slightly thickened.

3.   Meanwhile, blanch all the vegetables, each type individually, in simmering salted water, about 1 minute. Refresh in cold water, drain well, and set aside.

4. When the sauce has been reduced, add the vegetables and stir to heat through.

5. Add salt to the pot of boiling water and cook the bow ties until they are al dente, following the directions on the package. Drain the pasta and stir it into the sauce, coating well. Remove the skillet from the heat and stir in the grated cheese.

6. To serve, divide the pasta and vegetables among 4 large warm plates or bowls. Sprinkle each serving with some of the remaining chopped parsley and serve immediately.

TO PREPARE AHEAD: Through step 3, reheating the sauce on low heat.

CRISPY CALAMARI WITH CHINESE NOODLES AND SPICY GARLIC SAUCE

Most of our customers love fried calamari. For my Asian restaurant, Chinois On Main, I wanted to find a more interesting way to serve it besides as the usual appetizer. This dish is an alternative to those giant bowls of greasy fried squid! I like the contrast between the crunchy calamari and the soft, slightly spicy noodles.

Though this recipe appears long, don't be scared off. It's so easy to make. Prepare the sauce ahead of time, and when you're ready to eat, the only thing left to do is to cook the noodles and fry the calamari. To save time, have your fishmonger cut the squid into rings for you. The rice wine, rice wine vinegar, soy sauce, chili sauce, and Chinese egg noodles can be purchased at Asian markets and gourmet specialty stores.

SERVES 4

Oil for deep-frying

SAUCE

2 tablespoons peanut oil

³/4 cup (4 ounces) sliced Double-Blanched Garlic (see page 30)

2 tablespoons sugar

1 cup rice wine

¹/4 cup rice wine vinegar

2 tablespoons plus 1 teaspoon dark soy sauce

4 ounces carrots, peeled, trimmed, and cut into julienne (about 1 cup)

4 ounces haricots verts, trimmed, blanched, and refreshed (about 1 cup)

4 ounces green onions, trimmed and cut into strips (about 1 cup)

2 teaspoons Vietnamese chili sauce

12 ounces fresh Chinese egg noodles or thin spaghetti

1 pound calamari, cleaned and cut into ¹/4-inch rings

Kosher salt and freshly ground black pepper

About ¹/2 cup all-purpose flour

¹/4 teaspoon sesame oil

1.   Bring a large stockpot of water to a boil. In a wok or deep, heavy saucepan, heat about 3 inches of peanut oil. (The oil must be very hot, about 375°F.)

2.   Make the sauce: In a large skillet or sauté pan, heat the 2 tablespoons of peanut oil. Over medium-high heat, sauté the garlic just until golden, 2 to 3 minutes. Stir in the sugar and continue to sauté until the garlic begins to caramelize, 1 or 2 minutes longer. Deglaze the pan with the rice wine, rice wine vinegar, and soy sauce. Add the carrots, haricots verts, and 2 ounces of the scallions, reserving 1 ounce as garnish. Stir in the chili sauce and continue to cook until the sauce is reduced by half.

3.   Meanwhile, add salt to the boiling water and cook the noodles until they are al dente. Drain the noodles well and stir them into the sauce until they are well coated.

4.   Cook the calamari: Season the calamari with salt and pepper and toss with the flour to coat lightly. Deep-fry the calamari in small batches until golden, 1 or 2 minutes. (The easiest way to do this is to use a fine-mesh basket or strainer. Place the calamari in the basket and gently ease the basket into the oil.) Drain on clean paper towels.

5.   To serve, divide the noodles and vegetables among 4 large warm plates. Arrange the calamari over and around each portion and garnish with the remaining scallions. Drizzle a little sesame oil over the noodles and serve immediately.

TO PREPARE AHEAD: Through step 2, reheating the sauce over low heat.

The fried squid stays crispy when placed on top in one of our most popular pasta dishes: Crispy Calamari with Chinese Noodles and Spicy Garlic Sauce.

FETTUCCINE WITH FENNEL, OVEN-DRIED AND FRESH TOMATOES, AND NIÇOISE OLIVES

In southern California, fennel grows all year long. If you know where to look, you'll find it growing up in the hills, not far from the big Hollywood sign. If you're not as lucky as us Californians, fennel is usually available most of the year in the markets. The combination of oven-dried tomatoes with fresh tomatoes makes for a richer, sweeter sauce. And with the Niçoise olives, this is Provence on a plate.

SERVES 4

½ cup extra-virgin olive oil

¾ cup (4 ounces) sliced Double-Blanched Garlic (see page 30)

2 cups (5 ounces) thinly sliced fennel

1 cup (4 ounces) sliced Oven-Dried Tomatoes (see page 26)

1 cup (4 ounces) pitted Niçoise olives

2 teaspoons capers, drained

3 medium-size fresh tomatoes, peeled, seeded, and roughly chopped

2 tablespoons (¼ stick) unsalted butter

Pinch of sugar

Kosher salt and freshly ground black pepper

12 ounces fresh or store-bought fettuccine

2 tablespoons chopped fresh flat-leaf parsley leaves

2 tablespoons chopped fresh basil leaves, 2 tablespoons fresh basil leaves, cut into chiffonade for garnish

¼ cup freshly grated Parmesan cheese

1. Bring a large stockpot of water to a boil.

2. Reserving 2 teaspoons of the olive oil, heat the remainder of the ½ cup of oil in a large skillet. Sauté the garlic just until golden. Add the fennel, Oven-Dried Tomatoes, olives, and capers and cook over medium-high heat for 1 minute. Add the fresh tomatoes and stir to combine. Add the butter and sugar and cook until the juices are extracted from the tomatoes, about 3 minutes. Season to taste with salt and pepper.

3. Add salt to the boiling water and cook the fettuccine until it is al dente, about 1 minute for fresh pasta. (Cook packaged pasta according to the directions on the

box.) Drain the pasta well and stir it into the skillet, coating it thoroughly with the sauce. Remove from the heat and toss with the chopped parsely, basil, and the reserved 2 teaspoons of olive oil. (The oil will give the pasta a shine.)

4. To serve, divide the pasta and vegetables among 4 large warm plates or bowls. Sprinkle with the grated cheese and garnish with the basil chiffonade. Serve immediately.

TO PREPARE AHEAD: Through step 2, the sauce can be made about 1 hour before needed.

Fresh tomatoes often lose their flavor when added to a dish. The beauty of oven-dried tomatoes is that they are so concentrated in flavor and so rich in color.

FETTUCCINE WITH ROASTED RED PEPPERS

If you want a bit more color, you can use one red and one yellow bell pepper.

SERVES 2

2 tablespoons extra-virgin olive oil

1/4 cup chopped onion

2 tablespoons minced garlic

2 large red bell peppers (about
1 pound), roasted, peeled, cored,
seeded, and cut into 1/4-inch strips

Pinch of red pepper flakes

Kosher salt and freshly ground black
pepper

2/3 cup homemade Chicken Stock
(see page 4) or store-bought, heated

6 ounces fresh or store-bought
fettuccine

1 teaspoon chopped fresh thyme leaves

1/2 teaspoon sherry wine vinegar

Chopped fresh cilantro leaves, for
garnish

1.   In a medium skillet, heat the olive oil. Over medium-high heat, sauté the onions and garlic until translucent, 2 to 3 minutes. Stir in the roasted peppers and red pepper flakes and cook 3 to 4 minutes longer. Season with salt and pepper to taste. Remove about 1/4 of the mixture and reserve.

2.   Pour the stock into the pan with the remaining pepper mixture and bring to a boil. Transfer the ingredients to a blender and purée until smooth. Return to the pan and keep warm.

3.   Meanwhile, bring a large stockpot of water to a boil. Add a little salt and cook the noodles until they are al dente, about 1 minute for fresh pasta. (Cook packaged pasta according to the directions on the box.) Drain the noodles and stir them into the sauce. Stir in the chopped thyme, vinegar, and reserved roasted pepper mixture. Adjust the seasoning to taste.

4. To serve, arrange the pasta in the middle of 2 large heated plates or bowls, spooning additional sauce over each. Garnish with the chopped cilantro and serve immediately.

TO PREPARE AHEAD: Through step 2. When ready to serve, warm over low heat and then continue with the recipe.

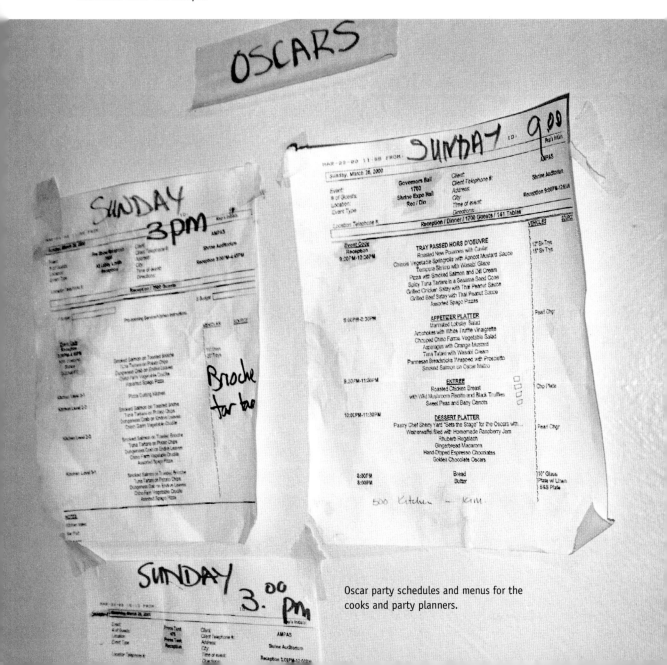

Oscar party schedules and menus for the cooks and party planners.

SPICY EGGPLANT FETTUCCINE

This is not for the faint-hearted. Cut down on the red pepper flakes if you prefer a less spicy variation. This colorful, tasty pasta is especially welcome when many of the summer vegetables are not available.

SERVES 4

3 Asian eggplants (about 1 pound), ends trimmed

¼ cup extra-virgin olive oil

Kosher salt and freshly ground white pepper

4 cloves sliced Double-Blanched Garlic (see page 30)

½ cup Oven-Dried Tomatoes (see page 26), cut into bite-size pieces

1 tablespoon chopped fresh rosemary leaves

1 teaspoon red pepper flakes

2 cups homemade Chicken Stock (see page 4) or store-bought, heated

12 ounces fresh or store-bought fettuccine

6 tablespoons (¾ stick) unsalted butter, cut into small pieces

2 tablespoons chopped fresh flat-leaf parsley leaves

4 ounces goat cheese, cut into pieces

6 fresh basil leaves, cut into chiffonade

1.   Cut the eggplant into ½-inch cubes. In a large sauté pan, heat the olive oil over medium heat. Add the eggplant, season lightly with salt and pepper, and cook until golden brown, on all sides. Add the garlic and sauté just until the garlic takes on a little color.

2.   Stir in the Oven-Dried Tomatoes, rosemary, and red pepper flakes and pour in the stock. Bring to a boil and let reduce until the sauce thickens slightly.

3.   Meanwhile, bring a large stockpot of water to a boil. Season with salt, and cook the pasta until it is al dente, about 1 minute for fresh pasta. (Cook packaged pasta according to directions on the box.) Drain the pasta well and add it to the sauce,

stirring to coat all the strands with the sauce. Stir in the butter, parsley, and goat cheese and adjust the seasoning to taste.

4.   To serve, divide the pasta among 4 large bowls and garnish with the chiffonade of basil. Serve immediately.

TO PREPARE AHEAD: The vegetables can be cut early in the day.

FETTUCCINE WITH LOBSTER AND GREEN CURRY SAUCE

If you prefer, steam the lobster first, remove the meat from the shell, reserve the meat, and use the shell for the sauce. Anaheim chilies give you the flavor of jalapeño without the heat. Plum wine and curry paste can be purchased in Asian markets and gourmet specialty stores.

SERVES 4

Two 1¼-pounds live lobsters

SAUCE

2 tablespoons extra-virgin olive oil

4 ounces fresh ginger, peeled and cut into small dice

2 large shallots (about 2 ounces), minced

6 medium garlic cloves, peeled and crushed

1 cup plum wine

1 cup dry white wine

1 tablespoon plus 1 teaspoon curry powder

1 tablespoon plus 1 teaspoon Thai green curry paste

2 cups homemade Chicken Stock (see page 4) or store-bought, heated

2 teaspoons brown sugar, packed

2 cups coconut milk

½ bunch green onions, with green stems, trimmed and cut into 1-inch lengths

½ cup fresh cilantro leaves

Kosher salt

14 ounces fettuccine

GARNISH

2 tablespoons (¼ stick) unsalted butter

2 ounces fresh shelled peas

1 Anaheim chili (about ¾ ounce), stemmed, seeded, and cut into thin rounds

1 medium carrot, peeled, trimmed, and cut into julienne

4 or 5 whole fresh basil leaves, or Thai basil, cut into chiffonade

Sprigs of fresh cilantro

Freshly ground white pepper

An array of cultures melds delightfully in Fettuccine with Lobster and Green Curry Sauce.

1.   Using a large, sharp knife, split each lobster lengthwise and crack the claws. Bring a large stockpot of water to a boil.

2.   Make the sauce: In a large saucepan, heat the 2 tablespoons of olive oil. Arrange the lobsters in the pan, flesh side down, and sear over high heat. Add the ginger, shallots, and garlic and cook until aromatic, about 2 minutes. Lower the heat, slowly pour in the plum and white wines, stir in the curry powder and curry paste, and reduce to a glaze, stirring occasionally.

3.   Pour in the stock and stir in the brown sugar. When the lobster meat is *almost* cooked, after about 2 to 3 minutes, remove it from the pan. Scoop out the meat and return the shells to the pan. Reduce the sauce until about ½ cup remains. Pour in the coconut milk and bring to a boil. Add the green onions and the cilantro leaves to the sauce and bring back to a boil. Remove the pan from the heat and let steep for about 10 minutes. Discard the lobster shells.

4.   Cut the lobster meat into bite-size pieces and reserve. Strain the sauce and reserve.

5.   When ready to serve, add salt to the pot of boiling water and cook the pasta until it is al dente, about 1 minute for fresh pasta, and drain. (Cook packaged pasta according to directions on the box.)

6.   Make the garnish: In a clean saucepan, melt the butter. Stir in the peas, Anaheim chili, and carrot. Pour in the strained sauce and bring to a boil. Add the drained pasta and the lobster meat and toss to combine thoroughly. Add basil and sprigs of cilantro, and stir into the sauce. Season with salt and pepper to taste.

7.   To serve, divide the pasta among 4 large heated plates or bowls. Spoon the sauce over and garnish with additional basil leaves, if desired.

TO PREPARE AHEAD: Through step 4, the sauce can be made a few hours before needed and reheated over low heat.

GNOCCHI WITH SAUTÉED WILD MUSHROOMS AND ROSEMARY SAUCE

Gnocchi are really very simple to prepare. You can shape them early in the day that you intend to serve them, cooking as needed. You can bake them as described below or in individual ovenproof dishes, serving them directly from the dish.

MAKES 72 GNOCCHI; SERVES 6 TO 8

GNOCCHI

1 recipe Potato Gnocchi (see page 121), cooked

1/2 cup freshly grated Parmesan cheese

SAUCE

2 tablespoons extra-virgin olive oil

1 large shallot (about 3 ounces), peeled and minced

3 or 4 garlic cloves, peeled and minced

1 cup dry white wine

2 cups homemade Chicken Stock (see page 4) or store-bought, heated

3 tablespoons unsalted butter, cut into small pieces

6 large Roma tomatoes (1 pound), peeled, seeded, and coarsely chopped

1/2 teaspoon minced fresh rosemary leaves

Kosher salt and freshly ground white pepper

SAUTÉED WILD MUSHROOMS

2 tablespoons extra-virgin olive oil

1/2 pound mixed wild mushrooms (such as shiitake, porcini, chanterelle), cleaned, trimmed, and cut into bite-size pieces

1 large shallot, peeled and minced

2 medium garlic cloves, peeled and minced

2 teaspoons chopped fresh flat-leaf parsley leaves

Kosher salt and freshly ground black pepper

1.   Make the sauce: In a medium saucepan, heat the olive oil. Over medium heat, sauté the shallot and garlic until translucent. Deglaze with the wine and reduce until

about ¼ cup remains. Pour in the stock and reduce by half. Remove from the heat and whisk in the butter. Stir in the tomatoes and the minced rosemary and season with salt and pepper to taste. Cool slightly and then transfer to a food processor or blender. Process to a partial puree, leaving some texture to the sauce. Set aside. When needed, reheat over low heat and adjust the seasoning to taste.

2. Prepare the mushrooms: In a medium skillet, heat the olive oil. Over medium heat, sauté the mushrooms until crisp-tender. Stir in the shallot, garlic, and parsley and cook 2 or 3 minutes longer. Season with salt and pepper to taste and set aside. When needed, reheat over low heat.

3. When ready to serve, preheat the oven to 350°F. and butter a 13 × 9 × 2-inch baking dish. Transfer the cooked gnocchi to the prepared dish. When the sauce is heated, pour the sauce over the gnocchi, sprinkle with the Parmesan cheese, and bake for about 10 minutes. To serve, gently spoon the gnocchi into warm soup plates, and scatter the mushrooms around the gnocchi.

TO PREPARE AHEAD: The gnocchi can be made up to two hours in advance, placed on a baking tray lined with parchment paper, lightly sprinkled with semolina or all-purpose flour, and kept at room temperature until ready to cook. The sauce and sautéed wild mushrooms can also be made early in the day and reheated as needed.

GNOCCHI WITH BRAISED VEAL SHANK

SERVES 4

———————————— ☀ ————————————

Four 22-ounce veal shanks

1 tablespoon kosher salt

1 teaspoon freshly ground black pepper

Flour, for dredging

1/4 cup extra-virgin olive oil

1 large carrot, peeled, trimmed, and cut into 1/2-inch round slices

1 medium onion, peeled, trimmed, and cut into 1-inch slices

2 stalks of celery, trimmed and cut into 1-inch slices

6 white button mushrooms, quartered

1/2 head of garlic, cut in half horizontally

1 Roma tomato, quartered

2 tablespoons tomato paste

1 1/2 cups dry white wine

3/4 cup red wine

3/4 cup port wine

2 whole bay leaves

2 sprigs fresh rosemary

4 sprigs fresh thyme

2 teaspoons whole black peppercorns

3 cups homemade Chicken Stock (see page 4) or store-bought

1 cup homemade Brown Veal Stock (see page 7)

4 tablespoons (1/2 stick) unsalted butter

1/2 recipe Potato Gnocchi (see page 121), cooked

1/4 cup freshly grated Parmesan cheese

4 sprigs of fresh rosemary, for garnish

1.   Preheat oven to 350°F.

2.   Prepare the veal shanks: Generously season the veal shanks with salt and pepper. Tie with kitchen twine and dredge in flour.

3.   In a large saucepan, over high heat, add two tablespoons of olive oil. Sear all sides of the veal shanks until brown. Remove the veal shanks and transfer to a tray. Reserve.

4. Add the remaining 2 tablespoons of olive oil. Add the carrot, onion, and celery. Sauté for 2 minutes or until golden. Add the mushrooms and garlic and continue to cook for another 2 minutes.

5. Add the tomato and tomato paste. Stir well to coat vegetables with tomato paste. Cook another 3 minutes.

6. Deglaze with the white, red, and port wines. Add the bay leaves, rosemary, 2 sprigs of thyme, and peppercorns. Bring to a boil and reduce until only ⅓ of the liquid remains.

7. Add the reserved veal shanks, 2½ cups of the chicken stock, and the veal stock. Bring to a boil. Turn off the heat, cover the pan, and transfer to the oven. Cook for 1½ to 2 hours or until fork tender.

8. Transfer the meat to a large sauté pan, strain the sauce, and add the remaining 2 sprigs of thyme and 2 tablespoons of butter. Over medium heat, continue to cook, on top of the burner, basting with the sauce every now and then, until the sauce starts to carmelize and coats the shank.

9. In another large sauté pan, bring the remaining ½ cup chicken stock and the remaining 2 tablespoons of butter to a boil. Add the cooked gnocchi and toss until coated with sauce. Stir in grated Parmesan cheese and season with salt and pepper.

10. To serve, divide the gnocchi into 4 heated plates, forming a 6-inch crown of dumplings in the center of each plate. Place a caramelized veal shank in the center of the crown. Place a sprig of rosemary inside the bone. Serve immediately.

PAPPARDELLE WITH GARLIC, OVEN-DRIED TOMATOES, AND HERBED GOAT CHEESE

I like the wider pasta with this very simple sauce, a combination of fresh and oven-dried tomatoes.

SERVES 3 TO 4

⅓ cup extra-virgin olive oil

3 tablespoons sliced Double-Blanched Garlic (see page 30)

⅓ cup Oven-Dried Tomatoes (see page 26), cut into large pieces

3 medium tomatoes (1½ pounds), peeled, seeded, and chopped

Kosher salt and freshly ground white pepper

12 ounces fresh regular or spinach pappardelle, or store-bought

4 ounces Herbed Goat Cheese (see page 26), cut into small pieces

6 to 8 large fresh basil leaves, cut into chiffonade

1.   In a 12-inch sauté pan or skillet, heat the olive oil. Lightly brown the garlic. Add the Oven-Dried Tomatoes and the chopped fresh tomatoes and season lightly with salt and pepper. Cook until the sauce has thickened slightly. Adjust the seasoning to taste.

2.   Meanwhile, bring a large stockpot of water to a boil. Add a large pinch of salt to the water and cook the pasta until it is al dente, about 1 minute for fresh pasta. (Cook packaged pasta according to the directions on the box.) Drain the pasta and combine with the sauce.

3.   To serve, divide the pasta and sauce among 3 or 4 large warm plates or bowls. Add the goat cheese and the basil chiffonade. Serve immediately.

TO PREPARE AHEAD: Through step 1, reheating over low heat when needed.

PAPPARDELLE WITH BEEF BOLOGNESE SAUCE

SERVES 4

4 tablespoons (½ stick) unsalted butter

6 tablespoons extra-virgin olive oil

2 cups Beef Bolognese Sauce
(see page 155)

½ cup homemade Chicken Stock (see
page 4) or store-bought

½ teaspoon minced fresh oregano
leaves

12 ounces fresh or store-bought
pappardelle

2 tablespoons minced fresh parsley
leaves

¼ cup freshly grated Parmesan cheese

Kosher salt and freshly ground black
pepper

Shaved Parmesan cheese, for garnish

1. Bring a large stockpot of salted water to a boil.

2. In a large sauté pan, over medium flame, heat all of the butter and 4 tablespoons of the olive oil. Stir in the Beef Bolognese Sauce, stock, and oregano. Bring to a slow boil, stirring constantly.

3. Meanwhile, cook the pappardelle until al dente and drain. Add to the sauce and stir to coat well. Stir in the parsley, grated Parmesan, and the remaining 2 tablespoons of olive oil. Season with salt and pepper.

4. To serve, divide the pasta among 4 heated plates or bowls. Garnish with shaved Parmesan cheese. Serve immediately.

BEEF BOLOGNESE SAUCE

MAKES 7 CUPS

6 tablespoons extra-virgin olive oil

1 pound lean ground beef

Kosher salt and freshly ground black pepper

2 teaspoons minced shallots

1 teaspoon minced garlic

½ cup dry red wine

5 pounds Roma tomatoes, cored, blanched, peeled, seeded, and chopped fine

2 tablespoons tomato paste

3 to 4 tablespoons sugar

1 sachet (2 sprigs fresh rosemary, 2 sprigs fresh basil, 1 sprig fresh oregano, 4 sprigs parsley, 2 bay leaves, 1 teaspoon black peppercorn, wrapped together in a cheesecloth, tied in a bundle)

1 medium onion (about 6 ounces), peeled, trimmed, and cut into fine dice

1 medium carrot (about 4 ounces), peeled, trimmed, and cut into fine dice

1 medium celery stalk (about 4 ounces), trimmed, and cut into fine dice

2 cups homemade Chicken Stock (see page 4) or store-bought

Sugar, to taste, optional

Red pepper flakes, optional

1.   In a large saucepan, heat 3 tablespoons olive oil. Add the ground beef and sauté until lightly browned, breaking up the pieces as they cook. Season with salt and pepper. Add the shallots and garlic and continue to cook until soft.

2.   Deglaze the pan with the red wine and reduce until almost dry.

3.   Add the tomatoes, tomato paste, sugar, and sachet. Bring to a boil, then lower to a simmer for 40 to 45 minutes, stirring every 5 minutes.

4. Meanwhile, in a small sauté pan, heat the remaining tablespoon of olive oil. Add the onion and carrot. Sauté for 1 minute. Add the celery and continue to cook another 1 to 2 minutes, until translucent. Season with salt and pepper.

5. Remove the sachet from the sauce and add the sautéed vegetables. Add the stock and simmer another 30 minutes. Season with salt, pepper, sugar, and red pepper flakes, if desired. Reserve and use as needed.

TO PREPARE AHEAD: Beef Bolognese Sauce can be prepared 2 to 3 days ahead and refrigerated until needed. It can be frozen up to 4 months.

PENNE WITH FRESH PEAS AND PROSCIUTTO

If the ingredients are readied early in the day, you can make the sauce while the pasta is cooking and have this dish on the table as soon as the pasta is al dente.

SERVES 4 TO 6

3 tablespoons extra-virgin olive oil

1/2 medium white onion (about 4 ounces), peeled, trimmed, and chopped fine

2 tablespoons pulp of whole Roasted Garlic (see page 32)

1 1/2 cups homemade Chicken Stock (see page 4) or store-bought, heated

1/4 cup freshly grated Parmesan cheese, plus more for garnish, if desired

3 ounces goat cheese, crumbled

4 tablespoons (1/2 stick) unsalted butter, cut into small pieces

1/2 teaspoon minced fresh oregano leaves

1/2 teaspoon minced fresh thyme leaves

Kosher salt and freshly ground white pepper

12 ounces penne (or tubular pasta of your choice)

2 cups shelled fresh peas (about 1/2 pound), blanched

1/2 cup Oven-Dried Tomatoes (see page 26), cut into strips

1/4 pound prosciutto, cut into thin strips

Chopped fresh flat-leaf parsley leaves, for garnish

1. Bring a large stockpot of water to a boil.

2. In a large sauté pan, heat the olive oil. Over medium heat, sauté the onions until golden. Add the garlic, pour in the stock, and stir in the Parmesan cheese, goat cheese, and butter. Cook just until the sauce thickens slightly. Season with the oregano, thyme, and salt and pepper to taste.

3. Meanwhile, cook the penne until al dente and drain. Add the penne to the sauce and stir to coat well. Stir in the peas and the tomatoes and cook 1 or 2 minutes

longer. Just before you are ready to serve, stir in the prosciutto and adjust the seasoning to taste.

4.   To serve, divide the pasta among 4 heated plates or bowls, making certain that you spoon some of the peas, tomatoes, prosciutto, and sauce over each serving. Garnish with the chopped parsley and grated Parmesan cheese, if desired. Serve immediately.

TO PREPARE AHEAD: Have all the ingredients ready, including the blanched peas, and continue with the recipe when ready to serve.

PENNE WITH CHICKEN, ASPARAGUS, OVEN-DRIED TOMATOES, AND PINE NUTS

This is a perfect way to use the tenderloin found on chicken breasts. The tenderloin may have to be cut in half rather than into cubes. Leftover chicken can also be used. If the chicken has been cooked, add it after the sauce has come to a boil in step 3, and continue with the recipe. Cut the asparagus the same length as the penne.

SERVES 4 TO 6

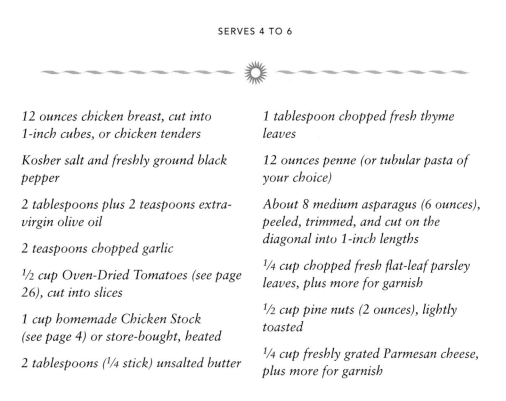

12 ounces chicken breast, cut into 1-inch cubes, or chicken tenders

Kosher salt and freshly ground black pepper

2 tablespoons plus 2 teaspoons extra-virgin olive oil

2 teaspoons chopped garlic

½ cup Oven-Dried Tomatoes (see page 26), cut into slices

1 cup homemade Chicken Stock (see page 4) or store-bought, heated

2 tablespoons (¼ stick) unsalted butter

1 tablespoon chopped fresh thyme leaves

12 ounces penne (or tubular pasta of your choice)

About 8 medium asparagus (6 ounces), peeled, trimmed, and cut on the diagonal into 1-inch lengths

¼ cup chopped fresh flat-leaf parsley leaves, plus more for garnish

½ cup pine nuts (2 ounces), lightly toasted

¼ cup freshly grated Parmesan cheese, plus more for garnish

1. Lightly season the chicken with salt and pepper and sprinkle with the 2 teaspoons of olive oil. Toss to combine and let the chicken marinate for 10 to 15 minutes.

2. Bring a large stockpot of water to a boil. Add a little salt into the water.

3. Heat a 12-inch sauté pan and then add the remaining 2 tablespoons of olive oil. When the oil is hot, add the chicken and, over medium heat, sear on both sides. Add the garlic and cook 1 minute longer. Stir in the tomatoes, add the stock, butter, and

thyme and bring to a boil. Season with salt and pepper to taste. Continue to cook until the sauce has reduced slightly.

4. Meanwhile, cook the pasta in the boiling water until it is al dente. Drain the pasta and immediately combine it with the sauce. Stir in the asparagus, parsley, and pine nuts, and toss to thoroughly combine the ingredients.

5. Remove the pan from the heat, sprinkle the Parmesan cheese over the pasta, and toss to combine. Adjust the seasoning to taste. You can also drizzle a bit of olive oil over the pasta to give it a shine.

6. To serve, divide the pasta among 4 to 6 large heated bowls. Garnish with additional chopped parsley and pass additional Parmesan cheese. Serve immediately.

TO PREPARE AHEAD: Through step 1. The marinated chicken can be refrigerated about 1 hour before needed.

PENNE WITH GLAZED SHALLOTS AND SAUTÉED MUSHROOMS

SERVES 4

¼ cup extra-virgin olive oil

4 ounces shiitake mushrooms, stemmed and cut into bite-size pieces

4 ounces oyster mushrooms, trimmed and cut into bite-size pieces

Kosher salt and freshly ground black pepper

¾ pound pencil asparagus, trimmed and cut into 2-inch pieces

3 cloves sliced Double-Blanched Garlic (see page 30)

Pinch of fresh chopped thyme leaves

Pinch of fresh chopped oregano leaves

1½ cups homemade Chicken Stock (see page 4) or store-bought, heated

½ cup Balsamic Glazed Shallots (see page 29)

6 tablespoons (¾ stick) unsalted butter, cut into small pieces

12 ounces penne (or any tubular pasta of your choice)

¼ cup freshly grated Parmesan cheese

7 or 8 fresh basil leaves, cut into chiffonade, for garnish

Shaved slices of Parmesan cheese, optional

1. Bring a large stockpot of salted water to a boil.

2. Heat a large sauté pan and add the ¼ cup of olive oil. Sauté the mushrooms until golden brown. Season with salt and pepper to taste.

3. Add the asparagus, garlic, thyme, and oregano. Pour in the stock, add the shallots, and reduce the sauce slightly. Whisk in the butter.

4. While the vegetables are sautéing, add the penne to the boiling water and cook until it is al dente, following the directions on the package. Drain the penne and stir it into the sauce, coating with the sauce. Stir in the grated Parmesan. Adjust the seasoning to taste.

5. To serve, divide the pasta and vegetables among 4 large bowls. Garnish with the basil and, if desired, shaved slices of Parmesan cheese. Serve immediately.

TO PREPARE AHEAD: The vegetables can be cleaned and cut early in the day.

A tribute to the country of Spain, this Saffron Risotto with Grilled Shrimp is sensual and enticing.

SAFFRON RISOTTO WITH GRILLED SHRIMP

6 tablespoons (³/₄ stick) unsalted butter

3 tablespoons extra-virgin olive oil

1 teaspoon minced garlic

1 teaspoon minced shallots

¹/₂ cup Arborio rice

Pinch of saffron threads

¹/₄ cup dry white wine

1 to 1¹/₂ cups homemade Chicken Stock
(see page 4) or store-bought, hot

¹/₄ cup freshly grated Parmesan cheese

Kosher salt

Freshly ground white pepper

8 large shrimp, peeled, deveined, and
halved lengthwise

¹/₂ teaspoon fresh lemon juice

Minced fresh parsley leaves

1. In a medium saucepan, heat 2 tablespoons each of butter and oil. Add the garlic and shallots and sauté until soft. Do not brown.

2. Add the rice and saffron and sauté until well coated with the oil.

3. Deglaze with wine and reduce until almost dry.

4. Using a 4-ounce ladle, add one ladle of boiling stock to the rice. Stir the rice over medium heat until the stock is absorbed and the rice is almost dry.

5. Add another ladle of stock and repeat the procedure until you have added all the stock or just until the rice is tender but still firm. It should be moist and creamy but not runny.

6. Remove from the heat and stir in the remaining 4 tablespoons of butter and the Parmesan cheese. Season with salt and pepper and add more stock if necessary.

7. Season the shrimp with 1 tablespoon oil, salt, and pepper. Cook over a hot grill just until done. Sprinkle with lemon juice and parsley. Divide the saffron risotto between 2 warm serving plates. Top each with half the grilled shrimp. Serve immediately.

SPRING RISOTTO

SERVES 4

⸻ ☀ ⸻

1 pound pencil asparagus, trimmed

4 ounces spinach, washed, dried, stemmed, blanched, liquid squeezed out

6 tablespoons (¾ stick) of unsalted butter

4 tablespoons extra-virgin olive oil

Kosher salt and freshly ground white pepper

1 tablespoon minced garlic

1 tablespoon minced shallots

¾ cup Arborio rice

⅓ cup dry white wine

2½ to 3 cups homemade Chicken Stock (see page 4) or store-bought, hot

½ cup freshly grated Parmesan cheese

Fried julienne of leeks, optional

1. Cut off 3-inch asparagus tips and reserve. Chop the remaining stalks, blanch, drain well, and transfer to a blender. Add the spinach and process to a purée. Pass through a fine-mesh strainer. Reserve. Blanch the asparagus tips, drain, and sauté in 1 tablespoon each of the butter and olive oil. Season with salt and pepper. Reserve.

2. In a medium saucepan, heat 3 tablespoons each of the butter and olive oil. Add the garlic and shallots and sauté until soft. Do not brown.

3. Add the rice and sauté until well coated with the oil.

4. Deglaze with the wine and reduce until almost dry.

5. Using a 4-ounce ladle, add one ladle of stock to the rice. Stir the rice over medium heat until the stock is absorbed and the rice is almost dry.

6. Add another ladle of stock and repeat the procedure until you have added a total of 2½ cups of stock, or just until the rice is tender but still firm.

7. Stir in the reserved vegetable purée.

8.   Remove from the heat and stir in the remaining 2 tablespoons of butter and the Parmesan cheese. Continue to add stock to the desired consistency. It should be moist and creamy but not runny. Season with salt and pepper.

9.   Divide among 4 heated serving plates and garnish with sautéed asparagus tips and fried julienne of leeks, if desired. Serve immediately.

ROASTED SQUAB ON PAN-FRIED NOODLES WITH SPICY MUSHROOM SAUCE

This has been on the menu at Chinois since the restaurant opened, twelve years ago. The crisp noodles, tender squab, and spicy sauce make this an unusual combination and often-requested dish. At the restaurant, we set the platter in the middle of the table for the guests to help themselves. Plum wine and rice wine vinegar can be purchased at Asian markets or gourmet specialty stores.

SERVES 2

✳

NOODLES

4 ounces Basic Pasta Dough
(see page 113) or 4 ounces Chinese
egg noodles

Salt

4 tablespoons peanut oil

SAUCE

1 tablespoon peanut oil

1 cup shiitake mushrooms, stems
reserved for soups or stocks

½ cup dry red wine

½ cup plum wine

½ cup Brown Chicken Stock (see page
5) or Brown Duck Stock (see page 8)

Kosher salt and freshly ground black
pepper

1 large garlic clove, minced

1 green onion, minced

¼ teaspoon minced fresh ginger

⅛ teaspoon red pepper flakes, chopped
very fine

One 1-pound squab

2 tablespoons peanut oil

1 bunch of fresh watercress, washed
and dried

½ tablespoon rice wine vinegar

2 teaspoons sesame oil

1.   Make the pan-fried noodles: Roll out the dough as thin as possible and, using a sharp knife or a pasta machine, cut into ¼-inch noodles. Bring a medium pot of water to a boil. Add a pinch of salt and cook the pasta until it is al dente. Rinse the pasta under cold water, drain well, spread it out on a tray lined with a clean towel, and dry thoroughly.

2. In an 8-inch nonstick skillet, over moderate heat, heat the peanut oil. Spread the noodles evenly over the pan and fry until the noodles are crisp and golden brown. Turn and brown the other side. The pancake should be crispy on the outside and still slightly soft on the inside. Set aside.

3. Preheat the grill or the oven to 400°F.

4. Make the sauce: In a 10-inch skillet, heat the tablespoon of peanut oil. Over medium-high heat, sauté the mushrooms for 2 or 3 minutes. Deglaze the pan with the red and plum wines and reduce to a glaze. Pour in the stock and reduce until the sauce thickens. Season lightly with salt and pepper. Keep warm. Just before serving, stir in the garlic, green onion, ginger, and red pepper flakes. Adjust the seasoning to taste.

5. Meanwhile, butterfly the squab and remove all but the leg bones. Season lightly with salt and pepper. In a skillet, heat 1 tablespoon peanut oil. Pan-sear the squab, skin-side down, for about 3 minutes, then turn and sear for 3 minutes longer. Finish skin-side down just to crisp. (To sauté, heat 1 tablespoon peanut oil in an ovenproof skillet. Brown both sides quickly and transfer to the oven. Roast at 400°F. for 10 to 12 minutes, or until medium rare.)

6. Prepare the watercress: In a small skillet, heat the remaining tablespoon of peanut oil. Sauté the watercress for 1 or 2 minutes, just to wilt. Stir in the rice wine vinegar and 1 teaspoon of sesame oil and season with salt and pepper to taste.

7. Separate the breasts, legs, and wings of the squab. Cut each breast into 4 slices. Reheat the pancake and cut it into four wedges.

8. Toss the watercress with the remaining teaspoon of sesame oil and arrange in the center of a large platter. Arrange the pancake wedges around the salad, points facing in, leaving a little space between each wedge. Place 2 slices of breast on each wedge and alternate the legs and wings around the wedges. Spoon the sauce over the squab and the wedges and serve immediately.

TO PREPARE AHEAD: Through step 2, the noodles can be prepared early in the day and re-heated at serving time in 1 tablespoon each peanut oil and butter. Through step 4, the sauce can be reheated over low heat. In step 5, you can have your butcher butterfly the squab and remove the bones.

SPICY THAI COLD NOODLES WITH CRUSHED PEANUTS AND CILANTRO

If using raw peanuts, drop the peanuts into about 1 inch of warm peanut oil and cook on low heat until they are lightly brown. (Nuts continue to cook even after they are taken out of the oil.) Drain on a clean towel. To make a complete meal of these noodles, surround them with cooked shrimp or lobster. At Spago, we often use mushroom soy sauce, which is darker and more concentrated than regular soy sauce, or combine the two. Mushroom soy sauce can be purchased in Asian markets or gourmet specialty stores.

SERVES 4

DRESSING

3 tablespoons light brown sugar

2 tablespoons plus 1 teaspoon soy sauce

2 tablespoons rice wine vinegar

1 tablespoon plus 1 teaspoon Chili and Garlic Oil (see page 20)

12 ounces fresh angel-hair pasta, cooked al dente, refreshed, and then allowed to dry*

1½ ounces Japanese pickled ginger, chopped (¼ cup)

¾ cup green onions, cut into 1-inch slices

½ cup fresh flat-leaf parsley leaves

1 Japanese cucumber, cut into julienne (½ cup)

1 small carrot, peeled, trimmed, and cut into julienne (¼ cup)

¼ cup roasted peanuts, coarsely chopped (1 ounce)

¼ cup minced fresh cilantro leaves

8 wedges of lime

1.   Make the dressing: In a small bowl, whisk together the sugar, soy sauce, vinegar, and Chili and Garlic Oil. Set aside.

---

*Fresh angel hair will cook in 1 minute. If using packaged pasta, follow the package directions for cooking. To dry the noodles, drain them well and then spread them out on a flat pan so that the noodles retain their shape and don't stick together.

2.   When the pasta is dry, place it in a large bowl and pour the dressing over. Toss to combine and let rest 1 or 2 minutes so that the dressing is absorbed. Add the remaining ingredients, reserving a few peanuts for garnish, and gently toss to combine.

3.   To serve, divide the pasta among 4 large bowls and garnish with the chopped peanuts, julienne of scallions, minced cilantro, and lime wedges.

1.

Pipe or spoon 1-teaspoon (approximately) mounds of filling, spaced 1 to 2 inches apart, along the egg-washed side of the dough.

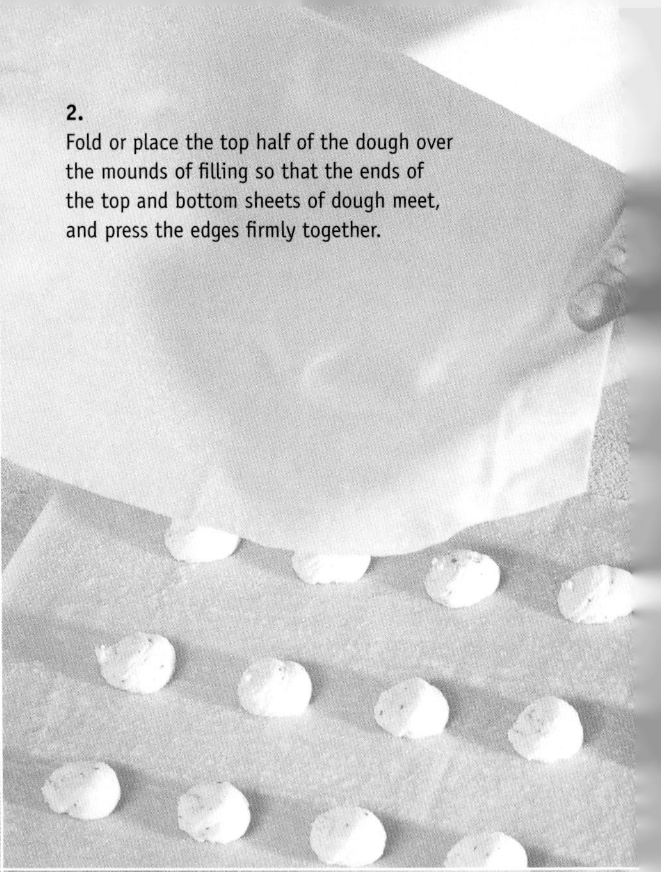

2.

Fold or place the top half of the dough over the mounds of filling so that the ends of the top and bottom sheets of dough meet, and press the edges firmly together.

3.

Using the outside edges of your hands, crimp around the mounds of filling.

4.

Cut out the ravioli with a round serrated cutter and place them on a floured surface.

mozz
the m

4. N
light
tang
need
the l
it co
1-in

5.

6.
ter.
tigh
che
Inv
bal
Th

7.
pl
sa

TC
u
r

Round ravioli: Place a teaspoon of filling on the right-hand side of the sheet of dough. Use a plain 3- to 4-inch round cutter to cut out the mound. Brush egg wash around the edges. Cut another round of dough and place on top, press top and bottom edges together to seal, and crimp around the filling.

Half-moon ravioli: Cut out and fill in the same manner as round ravioli but do not top with a second piece of dough. Brush egg wash on the outer edge and fold the circle in half over the filling, pressing the edges together to seal them.

Tortellini: Make a half-moon ravioli and then wrap it around your finger, pressing one end over the other to seal them together.

Cappelletti: To make a "little hat ravioli," use the round serrated cutter to cut out a 2-inch square of dough and place a teaspoon of filling in the center. Brush the edges with egg wash and fold two opposite corners together, sealing joined edges to form a triangle.

Wrap the triangle around your finger, pressing one end on top of the other to seal them together.

CHICKEN BOLOGNESE

This recipe should be made when tomatoes are at their peak of flavor. It makes a nourishing pasta sauce and freezes well, so you can have it at a moment's notice. The vegetables can be cut as described below, giving the sauce texture, or, if you prefer, they can be ground through a meat grinder or puréed in a blender or food processor for a smoother sauce. Serve it over linguine (see page 111) or with lasagne (see page 111).

MAKES ABOUT 5½ CUPS

5 tablespoons olive oil

2 pounds coarsely ground chicken, preferably dark meat

Kosher salt and freshly ground black pepper

1 medium white onion (about 2 cups), trimmed and cut into small dice

2 medium carrots (about 1 cup), trimmed, peeled, and cut into small dice

1 medium celery stalk, trimmed and cut into small dice

4 or 5 garlic cloves, cut into small dice

2 tablespoons tomato paste

1½ cups dry white wine

2½ pounds Roma tomatoes, peeled, seeded, and chopped fine

3 cups homemade Chicken Stock (see page 4) or store-bought, heated

Pinch of minced fresh oregano leaves

Pinch of minced fresh thyme leaves

6 or 7 chopped fresh basil leaves

Pinch of red pepper flakes, or to taste

1. In a 10- or 12-inch sauté pan, heat 3 tablespoons of the olive oil. Sauté the ground chicken until lightly browned, breaking up the pieces as they cook. Season lightly with salt and pepper. Remove the chicken with a slotted spoon and drain in a colander. Set aside until needed.

2. In the same sauté pan, heat the remaining 2 tablespoons of olive oil. Over medium heat, sauté the onion, carrots, and celery until they just start to color, 6 to 8 minutes. Do not brown. Add the garlic, stir in the tomato paste, and cook a few minutes longer.

3.   Deglaze the pan with the wine and cook, stirring occasionally, until almost all the liquid has evaporated. Add the tomatoes, cook for 2 or 3 minutes, then pour in the stock and season with the oregano, thyme, and a little salt and pepper. Cook until the sauce has thickened slightly, about 30 minutes. If the sauce has thickened too much or you prefer a thinner sauce, add a little more stock. Stir in the chopped basil and the red pepper flakes and adjust the seasoning to taste.

TO PREPARE AHEAD: Through step 3, the recipe can be prepared 1 or 2 days ahead and refrigerated until needed. It also can be frozen for up to 4 months.

CHICKEN LASAGNE

If you prefer, you can substitute 2 cups of *your* favorite tomato sauce. What makes this such a great Sunday-night favorite in our house is that almost any leftover meat—chicken, turkey, veal, or pork—can be used.

MAKES SIX 4-INCH LASAGNES OR ONE 9-INCH LASAGNE (SEE NOTE)

SAUCE

3 tablespoons extra-virgin olive oil

1/2 medium onion, peeled, trimmed, and diced

5 garlic cloves, peeled and minced

6 medium tomatoes (2 pounds), peeled, seeded, and diced

1 teaspoon diced jalapeño pepper, optional

1 teaspoon fresh thyme leaves

1 tablespoon chopped fresh basil leaves

Kosher salt and freshly ground black pepper

3/4 pound (1/2 recipe) Basic Pasta Dough (see page 113)

Semolina or all-purpose flour, for dusting

FILLING

1 pound spinach leaves, washed and stemmed but not dried

2 tablespoons extra-virgin olive oil

1 garlic clove, peeled and minced

Kosher salt and freshly ground black pepper

2 cups bite-size pieces of cooked chicken, turkey, or leftover roast, such as veal or pork

3 tablespoons freshly grated Parmesan cheese

1/2 cup mascarpone or cream cheese (4 ounces)

2 cups grated mozzarella cheese (8 ounces)

1/2 cup homemade Chicken Stock (see page 4) or store-bought, heated

1. Make the tomato sauce: In a large sauté pan, heat the olive oil. Over medium-high heat, sauté the onion and garlic until translucent, 3 to 4 minutes. Stir in the

tomatoes, jalapeño, thyme, and basil, lower the heat, and cook until the sauce thickens, about 15 minutes. Season with salt and pepper to taste and set aside. You should have about 2 cups of sauce.

2.   Prepare the pasta and cut into 3 pieces, 4 ounces each. Lightly sprinkle the work surface with flour. Using a pasta machine, rolling pin, or a combination of both, roll out one piece of dough as thin as possible and large enough to cut out eight 4-inch circles. Using a 4-inch cookie cutter, cut out 8 circles of dough. (Scraps can be folded and reworked as necessary.) Repeat with the remaining pieces of dough, and as the circles are cut out, transfer them to a baking tray lightly dusted with flour. You should have 24 circles of dough.

3.   Bring to a boil a large pot of water. Lightly salt the water, and cook the pasta circles, a few at a time, until al dente, about 1 minute. Remove with a slotted spoon, rinse under cold water, and set on a clean, dry towel until ready to assemble the lasagne.

4.   Make the filling: Cook the spinach with the water that clings to the leaves after washing, just until wilted. Drain thoroughly, and coarsely chop. In a small skillet, heat the 2 tablespoons of olive oil. Add the garlic and sauté briefly. Add the spinach and sauté just until the spinach is coated with the oil and garlic. Season lightly with salt and pepper and set aside.

5.   In a small bowl, combine the chicken with 3 tablespoons of the tomato sauce and 1 tablespoon of the grated Parmesan cheese. Season generously with black pepper and salt to taste.

6.   Preheat the oven to 400°F. Oil a baking tray and the inside of six 4-inch tart rings. Arrange the rings on the tray.

7.   To assemble each lasagna, press a pasta circle into one of the rings. Spread some of the mascarpone evenly over the circle and cover with a layer of the sautéed spinach. Top with a second circle and spread with a layer of the chicken mixture. Top with a third circle, spoon a little tomato sauce (1½ to 2 tablespoons) over, and cover with a final circle of pasta. Sprinkle with mozzarella and a little Parmesan cheese. Repeat with the remaining rings, pasta circles, mascarpone, spinach, chicken, sauce, mozzarella, and Parmesan cheeses. (At this point, the lasagnes can be

refrigerated. Remove them from the refrigerator 30 minutes before you are ready to bake them.)

8.   Bake until the cheese has melted and the lasagne is nicely browned, 20 to 25 minutes.

9.   Pour the stock into the reserved sauce and heat, stirring to combine. Adjust the seasoning to taste.

10.   To serve, spoon a little of the tomato sauce in the center of 6 warm dinner plates. Place each lasagne on the sauce and carefully remove the rings, using a small knife as necessary to cut around the dough. Serve immediately.

TO PREPARE AHEAD: Through step 7.

NOTE: To make one 9-inch lasagna, cut the pasta dough into 4 pieces, 3 ounces each. Roll out each piece as thin as possible and large enough to cut out a 9-inch circle. Using a 9-inch flan ring as a guide, cut out a 9-inch circle and repeat with the remaining pieces of dough. Cook the circles 4 to 5 minutes and proceed as above, layering with a pasta circle, mascarpone, spinach, a second pasta circle, the chicken mixture, a third circle, 1 cup of tomato sauce, the final circle, and the mozzarella and Parmesan cheeses. Bake 30 to 35 minutes. Cut into wedges and serve as above.

DUCK RAVIOLI WITH ROASTED RED PEPPER SAUCE

The brown stock, which can be made with duck or chicken, gives a distinct flavor and character to the sauce. If time is limited, stock can usually be purchased, frozen or fresh, at a gourmet shop.

MAKES 36 RAVIOLI; SERVES 6 TO 8

MOUSSE

1 teaspoon extra-virgin olive oil

½ medium red bell pepper, cored, seeded, and minced (about 3 ounces)

8 ounces boned and skinned chicken leg, cut into 1-inch pieces

6 ounces boned and skinned duck meat, cut into 1-inch pieces

¼ cup loosely packed chopped fresh chervil leaves

½ teaspoon kosher salt

½ teaspoon freshly ground white pepper

1 egg

1 cup heavy cream, chilled

1 pound Herb Pasta Dough (see page 115), cut into 4 pieces, about 4 ounces each

Semolina or all-purpose flour, for dusting

1 egg, lightly beaten with a little water, for egg wash

SAUCE

2 whole red bell peppers (about 1 pound)

1 tablespoon extra-virgin olive oil

2 garlic cloves, peeled and crushed

2 teaspoons red pepper flakes

2 or 3 Roma tomatoes (½ pound), peeled, seeded, and coarsely chopped

½ cup homemade Brown Duck Stock (see page 8) or Brown Chicken Stock (see page 5) or store-bought

1 cup heavy cream

3 tablespoons unsalted butter, at room temperature

2 ounces boned and skinned duck meat, cut into julienne

Kosher salt and freshly ground white pepper

Chopped fresh herbs, for garnish

1.   Make the mousse: In a small skillet, heat the olive oil. Over medium-high heat, sauté the red pepper, stirring occasionally, for 4 to 5 minutes. Cool *completely*.

2.   Chill the bowl and steel blade of the food processor. Combine the chicken and duck meat, chervil, salt, and pepper, and process with pulses until chopped. Add the egg and continue to process until puréed. With the motor running, pour the cream through the feed tube and process until the mixture is smooth, stopping the machine and scraping down the sides of the bowl as necessary. Transfer the mixture to a mixing bowl and fold in the cooled peppers. To test for taste, drop a teaspoonful of the mousse into simmering salted water and cook for about 2 minutes. Adjust the seasoning to taste. Refrigerate the mousse, covered, until needed.

3.   With a pasta machine or by hand, on a surface dusted lightly with flour, roll out one piece of the pasta dough, keeping the remaining pieces covered. Cut the dough into strips 3 inches wide by 16 to 18 inches long. Brush each strip of dough with egg wash and spoon about 1 tablespoon of filling at 2 to 2½-inch intervals along the bottom half. Fold the top half over to cover the mounds and press down around each mound to secure the filling. With a round (about 3-inch) cookie cutter, use half the cutter to cut into half-moon ravioli (see photo on page 171). Sprinkle flour on a baking tray, arrange the ravioli on the tray, and again sprinkle with flour. Repeat this procedure with the remaining pieces of dough, egg wash, and mousse. Refrigerate on a flour-dusted tray, covered, until needed.

4.   Make the sauce: Roast the peppers over an open flame or on a grill until the skin is blackened all over. Place the pepper in a paper bag, close the bag, and let the pepper steam for about 10 minutes. Remove the pepper and peel away the charred skin. Core and seed the pepper, pat it dry, and cut into strips.

5.   In a 10-inch skillet, heat the olive oil. Add the garlic cloves and red pepper flakes and cook 1 to 2 minutes. Do not brown the garlic. Stir in the roasted peppers and sauté 2 to 3 minutes. Add the tomatoes and cook 5 minutes longer, stirring occasionally. Pour in the stock and reduce just until thickened slightly. Pour in the cream, bring to a boil, and simmer 1 or 2 minutes. Scrape into a blender or food processor and purée. Strain into a clean saucepan, pressing down on the solids to get as much sauce as possible.

6. Meanwhile, in a small skillet, melt 1 tablespoon of the butter. Sauté the julienned duck over high heat until cooked on the outside but pink inside, 2 to 3 minutes. Whisk the duck into the sauce with the remaining 2 tablespoons of butter and season to taste with salt and white pepper.

7. When ready to serve, bring a large pot of water to a boil. Add salt to the water and then add the ravioli. Cook for 5 to 6 minutes. At the same time, heat the sauce over very low heat. Remove the ravioli with a slotted spoon and drain on a clean towel. Arrange the ravioli in the sauce and simmer until heated through, 2 to 3 minutes.

8. To serve, divide the ravioli among 6 or 8 large heated soup bowls. Spoon the sauce over with some of the julienned duck. Sprinkle with chopped herbs and serve immediately.

TO PREPARE AHEAD: In step 5, strain the sauce into a clean saucepan and continue with the recipe when ready to serve. Sauce can be made up to 2 days in advance and reheated.

MUSHROOM RAVIOLI

The mushrooms can be minced with a sharp knife or pulsed in a food processor. If using a food processor, first coarsely chop the mushrooms and then finish the job in the processor.

MAKES 24 RAVIOLI; SERVES 5 TO 6

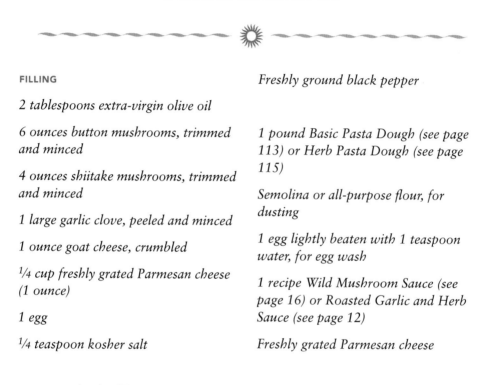

FILLING

2 tablespoons extra-virgin olive oil

6 ounces button mushrooms, trimmed and minced

4 ounces shiitake mushrooms, trimmed and minced

1 large garlic clove, peeled and minced

1 ounce goat cheese, crumbled

1/4 cup freshly grated Parmesan cheese (1 ounce)

1 egg

1/4 teaspoon kosher salt

Freshly ground black pepper

1 pound Basic Pasta Dough (see page 113) or Herb Pasta Dough (see page 115)

Semolina or all-purpose flour, for dusting

1 egg lightly beaten with 1 teaspoon water, for egg wash

1 recipe Wild Mushroom Sauce (see page 16) or Roasted Garlic and Herb Sauce (see page 12)

Freshly grated Parmesan cheese

1. To make the filling: Heat a 12-inch sauté pan and add the olive oil. Stir in the mushrooms and garlic, and over medium heat cook until most of the liquid is extracted from the mushrooms, about 10 minutes. Transfer to a medium bowl and let cool.

2. Stir in the remaining filling ingredients, and adjust the salt and pepper to taste. Refrigerate until needed.

3. Cut the pasta dough into 4 portions and work with 1 portion at a time, keeping the others covered with plastic wrap. Lightly dust the work surface with flour. With a pasta machine or a rolling pin, roll out the dough approximately 20 inches long

and 4 inches wide. Brush the dough with egg wash and spoon out 6 heaping table-spoons of filling along the bottom half of the length of the dough, about 2 to 2½ inches apart. Fold the top half over to cover the mounds of filling. Push the mounds toward the closed end of the dough and press down around each mound to secure the filling, making sure that you do not have any air pockets in any mounds. With a 2½-inch round cookie cutter, cut the ravioli into half-moon shapes. Dust a tray with flour and arrange the ravioli on the tray, dusting the ravioli with more flour. Repeat with the remaining dough, egg wash, and filling. Refrigerate, covered, until needed.

4.   Prepare the sauce and keep it warm.

5.   Bring a large pot of salted water to a boil. Cook the ravioli until al dente, about 3 to 4 minutes. Remove with a slotted spoon and add to the warm sauce, toss, and simmer for 1 minute.

6.   To serve, divide the ravioli among 5 to 6 heated plates or pasta bowls. Sprinkle with cheese.

TO PREPARE AHEAD: Through step 3. Ravioli will keep 1 day in the refrigerator.

POTATO, ROASTED GARLIC, AND BASIL RAVIOLI

MAKES 36 TO 40 RAVIOLI; SERVES 5 TO 6

FILLING (MAKES ABOUT 20 OUNCES)

1½ pounds baking potatoes, peeled and quartered (about 2 large)

¾ teaspoon kosher salt

½ cup Roasted Garlic (see page 32)

1 egg, lightly beaten

2½ tablespoons minced fresh basil leaves

2 tablespoons minced fresh chives

2 tablespoons freshly grated Parmesan cheese

½ teaspoon freshly ground white pepper

1 recipe Basic Pasta Dough (see page 113)

Semolina or all-purpose flour, for dusting

1 egg lightly beaten with 1 teaspoon water, for egg wash

1 recipe Roasted Garlic and Herb Sauce (see page 12)

¼ cup homemade Chicken Stock (see page 4) or store-bought

Kosher salt and freshly ground white pepper

Freshly grated Parmesan cheese

1.   Make the filling: Cook the potatoes in boiling salted water until tender, about 15 to 20 minutes. Drain. In a medium bowl, combine the potatoes and Roasted Garlic. Pass through a food mill on the fine setting. Add the remaining ingredients and stir until well blended. Cover and refrigerate until ready to use.

2.   Cut the pasta dough into 4 portions and work with 1 portion at a time, keeping the remaining dough covered with plastic wrap. Lightly dust the work surface with flour. With a pasta machine or a rolling pin, roll out the dough about 20 inches long and 4 inches wide. Brush the dough with the egg wash and spoon out 9 to 10 heaping tablespoons of filling along the bottom half of the length of dough, about 1 to 1½ inches apart. Fold the top half over to cover the mounds. Press down the dough around each mound to seal, making sure that you do not have any air pockets. Cut

into 2 × 2-inch squares. Dust a tray with flour and arrange the ravioli on the tray, dusting the ravioli with more flour. Repeat with the remaining three quarters of the dough, egg wash, and filling. Refrigerate, covered, until needed.

3.   Bring a large pot of salted water to a boil. Cook the ravioli until al dente, about 3 to 4 minutes.

4.   In a large sauté pan, reheat the Roasted Garlic and Herb Sauce (if too thick, add ¼ cup stock). Drain the ravioli and add them to the sauce, tossing to coat all sides. Add the cheese and season with salt and pepper. Serve immediately.

MY GRANDMA'S RAVIOLI

MAKES 36 TO 40 RAVIOLI; SERVES 5 TO 6

FILLING

*1 pound baking potatoes
(about 2 large), scrubbed thoroughly*

2 tablespoons (¼ stick) unsalted butter

2 tablespoons minced shallots

1 teaspoon minced garlic

8 ounces farmer cheese

5 ounces goat cheese

2 ounces mascarpone cheese

*3 tablespoons freshly grated Parmesan
cheese*

2 tablespoons minced fresh mint leaves

*2 tablespoons minced fresh chervil
leaves*

1 egg, lightly beaten

*Kosher salt and freshly ground white
pepper*

*1 recipe Basic Pasta Dough (see page
113)*

*Semolina or all-purpose flour, for
dusting*

*1 egg lightly beaten with 1 teaspoon
water, for egg wash*

8 tablespoons (1 stick) unsalted butter

¼ cup freshly grated Parmesan cheese

*Kosher salt and freshly ground white
pepper*

Minced fresh flat-leaf parsley leaves

1. Make the filling: Bake the potatoes in a preheated 350°F. oven until fork tender, about 30 to 40 minutes. Peel, and while still warm, pass through a food mill. In a small sauté pan, heat the butter over medium heat. Add the shallots and garlic, and cook until soft. In a medium bowl, combine all the cheeses, the herbs, and the beaten egg. Add the cooked shallots and garlic and the warm potato. Stir until blended (being careful not to overmix, or the mixture will get pasty). Season with salt and pepper. Cover and refrigerate until needed. Then, with lightly moistened hands, roll into ½-ounce balls, about the size of golf balls.

2.   Cut the pasta dough into 4 portions and work with 1 portion at a time, keeping the remaining dough covered with plastic wrap. Lightly dust the work surface with flour. With a pasta machine or a rolling pin, roll out the dough about 20 inches long and 4 inches wide. Brush the dough with egg wash and arrange 9 to 10 balls of filling on the lower third of the length of the dough, about 1 to 1½ inches apart. Fold the top half over to cover the balls. Press the dough around each ball to seal, making sure that you do not have any air pockets. With a 2-inch round cookie cutter, cut the ravioli. Dust a tray with flour and arrange the ravioli on the tray, dusting with more flour. Repeat with the remaining dough, egg wash, and filling. Refrigerate, covered, until needed.

3.   Bring a large pot of salted water to a boil. Cook the ravioli until al dente, about 3 to 4 minutes.

4.   Meanwhile, in a large sauté pan, over high heat, cook the butter until it begins to brown. Drain the ravioli and toss into the browned butter, turning to coat both sides. Add the cheese and season with salt and pepper. Garnish with parsley and serve immediately.

SMOKED SALMON RAVIOLI
WITH LIME-DILL BUTTER SAUCE

MAKES 32 RAVIOLI; SERVES 4 TO 6

MOUSSE

¼ pound smoked salmon, cut into 1-inch pieces

¼ pound fresh salmon, cut into 1-inch pieces

2 teaspoons coarsely chopped fresh dill

1 egg

½ cup heavy cream, chilled

½ teaspoon freshly ground white pepper

Kosher salt

Dash of cayenne pepper

½ recipe (12 ounces) Basic Pasta Dough (see page 113) or Herb Pasta Dough (see page 115)

Semolina or all-purpose flour, for dusting

1 egg, lightly beaten with 1 teaspoon water, for egg wash

SAUCE

¾ cup dry white wine

Juice of 1 medium lime, plus more to taste

1 tablespoon minced shallot

1 cup homemade Chicken Stock (see page 4) or store-bought, heated

½ cup heavy cream

6 tablespoons (¾ stick) unsalted butter, at room temperature, cut into small pieces

¼ cup chopped fresh dill, plus sprigs of dill for garnish

Kosher salt and freshly ground white pepper

1 red bell pepper, roasted, cored, peeled, seeded, and cut into julienne

1. Make the mousse: Chill the bowl and blade of a food processor. Process the smoked salmon, fresh salmon, and dill with a few pulses. Add the egg, and, with the machine running, pour the cream through the feed tube and process until the mix-

ture is a smooth purée. Transfer to a small bowl and season with salt, white pepper, and cayenne to taste. Cover and refrigerate until needed.

2.   Cut the pasta dough into 4 equal pieces. Working with 1 piece at a time, keep the remaining pieces covered. Using a pasta machine or by hand, on a surface dusted lightly with flour, roll out the first piece of dough to a rectangle, about 28 inches long and 6 inches wide, trimming as necessary. (See page 114 about working with smaller lengths of dough if desired.) Brush the dough with egg wash and, using a heaping teaspoonful of the mousse for each mound, place 16 mounds on the dough at 1½-inch intervals in two rows, one row about 1 inch from the top and the second row about 1 inch from the bottom. Roll out the second piece of dough and cover, pressing down around each mound to secure the filling. With a sharp knife or pizza cutter, cut the ravioli into approximately 3-inch squares, trimming the edges as necessary. Arrange on a tray dusted with flour. Repeat with the remaining dough, egg wash, and mousse. Refrigerate, covered, until needed.

3.   While preparing the sauce, bring a large pot of water to a boil.

4.   Make the sauce: In a medium saucepan, reduce the wine, lime juice, and shallot until ¼ cup liquid remains. Pour in the stock and reduce by half. Pour in the cream and reduce just until the sauce thickens. Strain, pressing down on the shallots to get all the sauce, and return to a clean pan. Whisk in the butter and dill and season with salt and white pepper to taste. Keep warm.

5.   Add a little salt to the pot of boiling water, then add the ravioli and cook for 5 minutes. Drain the ravioli on a clean towel and place in the sauce with the julienned bell pepper. Over low heat, reheat the ravioli.

6.   Divide the ravioli among 4 to 6 heated plates. Spoon the sauce over and garnish with a sprig of dill, if desired. Serve immediately.

TO PREPARE AHEAD: Through step 4. The ravioli and the sauce can be prepared early in the day. The sauce can be reheated over very low heat. If the sauce thickens too much, thin with a little stock.

SPINACH AND WILD MUSHROOM RAVIOLI

MAKES 36 TO 40 RAVIOLI; SERVES 5 TO 6

FILLING (MAKES ABOUT 20 OUNCES)

3 tablespoons extra-virgin olive oil

2 tablespoons (¼ stick unsalted butter)

6 ounces spinach, washed, dried, and stemmed

10 ounces shiitake mushrooms, stems removed, cut into bite-size pieces

6 ounces oyster mushrooms, trimmed, cut into bite-size pieces

1 tablespoon minced shallots

2 teaspoons minced garlic

¾ teaspoon kosher salt

Freshly ground black pepper

1 egg

½ cup fresh bread crumbs

1 tablespoon minced fresh parsley leaves

1 teaspoon minced fresh thyme leaves

1½ tablespoons freshly grated Parmesan cheese

1 recipe Basic Pasta Dough (see page 113)

Semolina or all-purpose flour, for dusting

1 egg lightly beaten with 1 teaspoon water, for egg wash

1 recipe Wild Mushroom Sauce (see page 16)

Kosher salt and freshly ground pepper

¼ cup homemade Chicken Stock (see page 4) or store-bought

Minced fresh flat-leaf parsley leaves

Freshly grated Parmesan cheese

1. Make the filling: In a large sauté pan, heat 1 tablespoon of the olive oil and the butter. Add the spinach and cook over high heat just until wilted, about 2 minutes. Drain and coarsely chop. Set aside. Wipe the pan.

2. In the same pan, heat the remaining 2 tablespoons of olive oil. Over high heat, sauté the mushrooms until tender, 2 to 3 minutes. Add the shallots, garlic, salt, and pepper. Sauté another minute. Transfer to a food processor fitted with the steel

blade, add the chopped spinach, and process until smooth. Add the remaining ingredients and continue to process until well incorporated. Transfer to a bowl, cover, and refrigerate until well chilled.

3.   Cut the pasta dough into 4 portions and work with 1 portion at a time, keeping the remaining dough covered with plastic wrap. Lightly dust the work surface with flour. With a pasta machine or a rolling pin, roll out the dough about 20 inches long and 4 inches wide. Brush the dough with egg wash and spoon out 9 to 10 heaping tablespoons of filling along the bottom half of the length of dough, about 1 to 1½ inches apart. Fold the top half over to cover the mounds of filling. Press down around each mound to seal, making sure that you do not have any air pockets. With a 2-inch round cookie cutter, shape the ravioli. Sprinkle a tray with flour and arrange the ravioli on the tray, dusting the ravioli with more flour. Repeat with the remaining dough, egg wash, and filling. Refrigerate, covered, until needed.

4.   Bring a large pot of salted water to a boil. Cook the ravioli until al dente, about 3 to 4 minutes.

5.   In a large sauté pan, reheat the Wild Mushroom Sauce (if too thick, add ¼ cup stock). Drain the pasta and add to the sauce, tossing to coat all sides. Add the cheese and season with salt and pepper, garnish with minced parsley, and serve immediately.

TO PREPARE AHEAD: Through step 3. Ravioli will keep 1 day in the refrigerator.

SWEET POTATO RAVIOLI WITH HAZELNUT BROWN BUTTER AND HERB SAUCE

When sweet potatoes are not available, kabocha (Japanese pumpkins) are a good substitute. Kabocha should feel firm and heavy for their size. Look for hard skin free of cracks and soft spots. Slight variations in skin color are natural and acceptable.

MAKES 36 TO 40 RAVIOLI; SERVES 6

FILLING (MAKES ABOUT 20 OUNCES)

1¼ pounds red jewel yams, scrubbed clean, peeled, and cut into chunks

2 ounces goat cheese

1½ ounces pine nuts, lightly toasted

¼ cup freshly grated Parmesan cheese

1 teaspoon minced fresh sage leaves

½ teaspoon minced fresh rosemary leaves

½ teaspoon kosher salt

1 tablespoon honey

1 egg, lightly beaten

1 recipe Basic Pasta Dough (see page 113)

Semolina or all-purpose flour, for dusting

1 egg lightly beaten with 1 teaspoon water, for egg wash

1 recipe Hazelnut Brown Butter and Herb Sauce (see page 10)

Kosher salt and freshly ground white pepper

Freshly grated Parmesan cheese

Fried sage leaves, for garnish

1. Make the filling: In a medium saucepan, cover the yams with cold water and bring to a boil. Cook until yams are fork tender. Drain well and pass through a food mill on the medium setting into a medium bowl. While they are still warm, stir in all the remaining ingredients except the egg. Cool to room temperature and stir in the egg. Refrigerate covered for 2 hours before forming the ravioli. (It is best used when cold.)

2.   Cut the pasta dough into 4 portions and work with 1 portion at a time, keeping the remaining dough covered with plastic wrap. Lightly dust the work surface with flour. With a pasta machine or a rolling pin, roll out one piece of dough approximately 20 inches long and 4 inches wide. Brush the dough with egg wash and spoon out 7 heaping tablespoons of filling along the bottom half, about 2 to 2½ inches apart. Fold the top half over to cover the mounds of filling. Push the mounds toward the closed end of the dough and press down around each mound to secure the filling, making sure that you do not have any air pockets. With a 3-inch round cookie cutter, cut the ravioli into half-moon shapes. Dust a tray with flour and arrange the ravioli on the tray, dusting the ravioli with more flour. Repeat with the remaining dough, egg wash, and filling. Refrigerate, covered, until needed.

3.   When ready to serve, bring a large pot of salted water to a boil.

4.   Prepare the Hazelnut Brown Butter and Herb Sauce. Cook the ravioli until al dente, about 3 to 4 minutes. Remove the ravioli with a slotted spoon and add to the sauce, and simmer for 1 minute. Season with salt and pepper.

5.   To serve, divide the ravioli among 6 heated plates or pasta bowls. Sprinkle with cheese and garnish with fried sage leaves.

THREE-CHEESE RAVIOLI

The rich combination of the cheeses takes this ravioli out of the realm of the ordinary.

MAKES 20 TO 24 RAVIOLI; SERVES 4

FILLING

4 ounces goat cheese

2 ounces blue cheese

2 ounces (about 1/2 cup) freshly grated Parmesan cheese

1 small baking potato (about 4 ounces), baked, pulp removed from the shell and mashed

2 eggs

2 tablespoons minced fresh chervil leaves

2 tablespoons chopped fresh chives

Kosher salt and freshly ground white pepper

1/2 recipe (12 ounces) Basic Pasta Dough (see page 113)

Semolina or all-purpose flour, for dusting

1 egg, lightly beaten, for egg wash

SAUCE

1 cup homemade Chicken Stock (see page 4) or Vegetable Stock (see page 6) or store-bought

Kosher salt and freshly ground white pepper

8 tablespoons (1 stick) unsalted butter, at room temperature, cut into small pieces

3 tablespoons freshly grated Parmesan cheese

1 tablespoon chopped fresh chervil leaves

1 teaspoon chopped fresh sage leaves

1 teaspoon chopped fresh marjoram leaves

Sprigs of fresh chervil, for garnish

1. Make the filling: In a medium bowl, combine the goat cheese, blue cheese, grated Parmesan cheese, mashed potato, and eggs. Mix well. Stir in the 2 table-

spoons of chopped chervil and the chives, and season to taste with salt and pepper. Refrigerate in a covered bowl until needed.

2.   Cut the pasta dough in quarters. Work with one quarter at a time, keeping the other three quarters covered with a clean towel. Lightly dust the work surface with flour. With a machine or by hand, roll out the first piece of dough about 15 inches long and 4 inches wide, trimming as necessary. Brush the bottom half of the dough with egg wash and, using a heaping teaspoon of filling, spoon out 5 to 6 mounds of the filling at 2-inch intervals. Cover the mounds with the top half of the dough and then gently press down and around each mound to seal. With a round cookie cutter (about 2½-inch), using half the cutter, cut the ravioli into half-moon ravioli. (See photo on page 171.) Dust a tray with flour, preferably semolina flour, and arrange the ravioli on the tray. Sprinkle a little more flour over the ravioli. Repeat with the remaining dough, the remaining egg wash, and filling. Refrigerate, loosely covered with parchment paper, until needed.

3.   At serving time, while you make the sauce, bring a large stockpot of water to a boil.

4.   Make the sauce: In a saucepan wide enough to hold the sauce and ravioli, pour the stock into the pan. Season with salt and white pepper and bring to a boil. Whisk in the butter, a few pieces at a time, and cook just until slightly reduced. Keep warm.

5.   Add a little salt to the pot of boiling water and cook the ravioli in batches, for 3 to 4 minutes. Do not overcrowd the pot. As the ravioli are cooked, remove with a slotted spoon and drain on a clean towel.

6.   Stir the Parmesan cheese, chervil, sage, and marjoram into the sauce and season to taste with salt and pepper. Add the ravioli and let simmer for 1 or 2 minutes to finish cooking and to heat through.

7.   To serve, divide the ravioli among 4 heated bowls. Spoon the sauce over and garnish with a small sprig of chervil. Serve immediately.

TO PREPARE AHEAD: Through step 2.

INDEX

ABOUT THE AUTHOR

WOLFGANG PUCK is the chef and owner of a number of remarkable restaurants, including the famous Spago restaurants, Chinois on Main, Postrio, Granita, Trattoria del Lupo, and the Wolfgang Puck Cafés. He is the author of three previous cookbooks, among them the ever popular *Adventures in the Kitchen*. He appears regularly on *Good Morning America* and the Home Shopping Network. Puck lives in Los Angeles with his wife and partner, Barbara Lazaroff, and their two sons.